# Tool-Maker to God Maker:
# A Human Journey

## Edward Conklin Ph.D.

Copyright 2014 by Edward Conklin. All Rights Reserved.

This book or any portion thereof may not be reproduced or used in any manner including any electronic or mechanical information storage and retrieval systems, without the express permission of the publisher. Scanning, uploading, photocopying, and facilitating the electronic distribution of this book without permission of the publisher is prohibited. Brief quotations in a book review is permitted.

ISBN: 978-0-9906457-0-2

## Acknowledgement

I acknowledge and express a heartfelt thanks to family and friends, whose true importance I came to realize during the passage of years; thank you each for sharing the journey and mutual touching of hearts. I thank Ms. Natalie Harley for her patient assistance in the editing process. To my teacher and the teachers of days gone by, thank you for sharing your wisdom. I also gratefully acknowledge my Arya ancestors, noble forebears of long-ago India whose keen brilliance was ignited by Dravida forest seers, and their transcendent visions of heart and soul.

Edward Conklin

Published works by Edward Conklin Ph.D.

A Brief Guide to God and the Soul. (2015). Amazon Kindle and CreateSpace.

In the Beginning: A New Theory of the First Religion. (2014).

Cosmos, God, and Soul. (2014). Amazon Kindle and CreateSpace.

From Tool-maker to God Maker. (2014). Amazon Kindle and CreateSpace.

Waves Rough and Smooth & the Deep Blue Sea. (2014). Amazon Kindle and CreateSpace.

Getting Back Into the Garden of Eden. (1998). University Press of America.

Edward Conklin

## Contents

Acknowledgement ........................................................................... 3
Contents .......................................................................................... 7
Introduction .................................................................................... 9

Chapters

1. Memoir ................................................................................ 11-16
2. Early Thoughts .................................................................... 17-22
3. God Maker ........................................................................... 23-38
4. Prehistoric and Historic Beginnings ................................... 39-48
5. Judaism ................................................................................ 49-74
6. Christianity .......................................................................... 75-84
7. Islam .................................................................................... 85-92
8. Hinduism ............................................................................ 93-100
9. Taoism .............................................................................. 101-112
10. Heraclitus ........................................................................ 113-120
11. Buddha ............................................................................ 121-138
12. Schopenhauer .................................................................. 139-146
13. Metaphysical Views ....................................................... 147-178
14. Denouement .................................................................... 179-195

Edward Conklin

Introduction

In the early days of this work, I thought to use fictional characters for each chapter as a rhetorical device to speak through them. But then came the thought that this approach was merely a story to entertain, and this was not my intent at all. Only children and immature adults are in need of story and fiction, or need to be vicariously entertained. Life is much too serious and brief for a thinking person to seek only to be entertained. Besides, no form of fiction entertainment can compare to the reality show of daily existence. But how did this show come to be? Humankind has, through long historic evolution of cognitive ability, attempted to solve the riddle of existence by posing basic questions. Some of these questions are from what or where has the environment and life come from? What unseen presence moves life on the inside? What importance, if any, does human behavior have?

The following is an investigation and commentary on humankind's long evolutionary cognitive journey to answer a few important questions of existence. To solve a mystery, as many know, is very gratifying. To shed some light on the mystery of life existence is even more gratifying, and to share this light is the most gratifying experience of all. Therefore this work seeks to be a conversation with the reader. I have not recklessly thrown words and ideas around, and have not sought to be overly popular or academic in tone. I only seek to present what some of the wise sons of humans have seen through long years; to kindle a fire, to sit and share the light and warmth of their illuminating insights, and to share a few of my own.

Edward Conklin

# Chapter 1

*Know thyself.* Delphic Oracle

## Memoir

I have often found the life of a writer of words to be both interesting and relevant to what he or she has said; in this spirit I offer the following account. Beginning in early childhood I had an intense curiosity to comprehend existence, of where things came from, the miracle of how they functioned, why I was here on earth, and what happened if anything after death. I grew up in the scenic Catskill Mountains of upstate New York, and at an early age developed a rapport with nature. When finished with mandatory family chores, I spent many days of the passing seasons, alone or with friends, enjoying horses and dogs, trout fishing, and wandering through the woods, fields, streams, rock-ledges, abandoned farms and barns, and back country roads.

While young, I recall observing that adults often had feelings and thoughts they did not express, and so reality frequently seemed at times to be dreamlike to me. I often did not know what was more real, what I was seeing and hearing, or what I was sensing and feeling. Often as a child, I experienced an aesthetic swell of emotion that I was not able to put into words. It was a mixture of love, empathy, or a touch of sadness. I sometimes felt the fear of change, the strife of conflict, or the expected or unexpected death of my family dogs or relatives, especially my grandfathers. I was often caught in the middle of wanting to be away from bad and sad experiences, and wanting the good not to pass away. The contrast produced a poignant depth of ambivalent feeling within my young body and mind. I later related this childhood experience of sensitivity to the Japanese aesthetic of "mono no aware." This is a phrase used to describe a view of the world as a general awareness of the transience of things, and a gentle compassion and empathetic sadness at their passing.

When just a tender eighteen-month old, my father was away in WWII, and my mother and I lived with my grandmother and four young attractive aunts. One day, while crawling on the living room floor, my grandmother was speaking to someone, and did not notice as she inadvertently stepped on the pinky finger of my left hand. It was only later in life while meditating that I recalled this incident in vivid detail. I remembered the sudden pain of her shoe crushing my finger, crying, and my grandmother lifting me to her breast to comfort me. I remembered revulsion toward her as I somehow realized she was connected to the pain I felt so intensely. I was rescued by my young aunts, who, one by one, took me into their arms and soothed my anguish by kissing my finger, blowing on it, and babying me with their words. This early memory was the first time in my life (aside from the birthing process) that I had experienced any sort of intense physical pain and mental anguish. The experience, I think, was what motivated me to later explore and intently seek answers about the human condition. It was later, while in college, that I first heard about the teachings of Buddha who said that existence was prone to suffering. I felt like a light bulb had been turned on in my head. I remember thinking at the time that the Buddha was an honest man, and it encouraged me later to explore Buddhist teachings in more depth.

My parents were perfect, but they were so only for me. Had they been too nice, or had I lived a too comfortable life with them, I would have only been concerned with my own success in life. In contrast, had my parents been too harsh and mean, I would have been too traumatized to function sensitively and sanely. My parents were "just right" as Goldilocks exclaimed in the story, as they generated just the right amount of love, support, struggle, and conflict to arouse my curiosity to explore the mystery of the human condition. I also have several recollections of standing by the road near our house at age five or six, expectantly waiting for my real parents to come and take me home. I thought that the people I lived with were not my real parents, and at the time were just babysitting me. Later in life I suspected that this thinking and behavior at such a young age probably had something to do with reincarnation and unremembered past lives.

While attending Methodist Sunday school as a child of seven years, I recall hearing the first story of the Garden of Eden. My reaction, even at that early age, was to question the story and especially the character and behavior of the god. I remembered asking the woman instructor, "How could a parent god be so mean and punish the first young humans?" I was told the first humans were bad and had committed a sin by disobeying. Though young, I was instinctively skeptical, and felt no urgency to accept the simplistic story. So I disbelieved it. My later life seems to have been influenced by this particular early experience. I also remembered questioning my mother about the story, and feeling dissatisfied with her explanation as well.

Curious and sensitive to the ways of my small country world, I made my way out to the greater world. I dropped out of high school to work, but later joined the military for three years. With the assistance of the GI Bill, I completed my GED, attended four years of college and graduated with a degree in psychology. In my late twenties, I also began to practice meditation so as to better obtain both objective and subjective insight into how things are. I worked for six years in the mental health field, and later obtained my Master's degree in Humanities, majoring in philosophy and religion. I eventually began to teach on the college and university level and completed my Ph.D. focusing on the psychology of Religious Studies. By this stage in life, I felt qualified enough to undertake what I felt was a vague personal quest to comprehend life, existence, and some kind of wisdom.

Reaching middle-age years, I was curious and concerned only with the reality of existence. I had few hobbies that I can recall, did not care for entertainment or vicarious sports, read no newspapers (though I kept up with world news), and read very little fiction literature. I read mainly in the areas of philosophy, psychology, religion, and to a lesser extent science. Friends would often tell me I had a dry sense of humor. Perhaps so, for when asked "How is it going?" I usually replied, "It's always going, taking us right along with it; there's no getting off. I once attempted to get off, but it dragged me right back on."

At other times when someone inquired as to how I was doing, I often responded with, "Could be better or could be worse. It's the same old story; always ups and downs. It's the way it's always been." Friends were sometimes mildly amused when I remarked that I preferred not to "understand," as this was to stand under an object, person, or situation. I much more preferred to "overstand," or to look over carefully and to better comprehend.

Eventually in the fertile fields of my successes, the weeds of dissatisfaction unknowingly sprouted and began to grow. My marriage of eight years fell apart and I was thrown back on my own resources. I began to question existence even more than I had done so in the past. I cannot precisely identify when I began to be disillusioned, or when my illusions of life began to be removed, but it began with brief isolated thoughts. Gradually more and more insights came into awareness with increasing frequency and intensity. I began thinking about the strains and hassles of life. Why do we have the strain and hassle of getting from one place to another, or going from home to work and back at the end of the day? What about the strains and hassles of going on trips, or getting to restaurants or movies? Why all of this when the only true destination was eventual ageing and death?

The seemingly innocuous acts of everyday living like working, shopping, and eating that I had so long comfortably taken for granted became a burden. I had lost interest in entertainment or the news of the day. Life was not working, and I had no choice but to retreat from it—to drop out—at least for a while. Friends commented that I had probably developed an early case of a mid-life crisis. Due to my sequestered lifestyle of study at the time, the suspicion and joke in the family during the 1980's was that I was the then unknown "Unabomber."

I have spent much of my life investigating philosophical, religious, psychological, and scientific views that seek to plumb the depths of existence. I became intrigued in how religion and the sciences of cosmology and physics have differing views on the origin of existence; however, both religion and science agree that the ultimate cause cannot be directly observed.

Through investigation I found that the changes of relative earthly causes are often difficult to perceive and have knowledge of; how much more so the cosmic cause of all existence? Both religion and theoretical cosmology and science of physics have to settle for the study of the effects rather than a cosmic cause. Theistic religion promotes faith and belief in a human-like god. Religious mystics claim to experience the ultimate source of existence through visions and realizations but investigators and readers of these reports are often skeptical as the experiences are not available to empirical observation or to personal experience of another observer. In contrast, empirical science insists on sensory observation, measurement of various phenomena, and theorizing.

Through the years, views that do not rely on the view of a human-like god or the ineffable visions of mystics, as well as not having been the result of scientific experiment, have arisen and have been verbally expressed. These intuitive views developed through observation and contemplation of the behavior of environmental and living forms that have come from an unfathomable cosmic cause. Throughout historical times, various individuals, cultures, philosophies and religions have developed differing views of a cosmic cause, how things have come from it, and how the environment and life are connected to it. In general, the less advanced theistic religions are based on the projection of human attributes through innate perceptual processes known as animism and anthropomorphism, and the conceptual process of analogical reasoning. In contrast, the more cognitively astute religions and philosophies arrive at the attributes of a cosmic cause based on observation and intuitive experience.

Gazing on the mysterious universe in which all exists, there are amazing waves of harmony and rhythm of differing forms and function that are a marvel to contemplate. There exist as many, if not more, rough waves of reality that batter each and all, and destroy on uncountable occasions. Contemplating the rough and smooth surface waves of existence, has previously led others, and also myself, to ponder the depths of the universe upon which a multitude of limitless waves occur. In the chapters that follow I share with you, reader; glimpses of what I have found.

Edward Conklin

## Chapter 2

*So, life is a game in which what isn't, is more important than what is. Werner Erhard*

### Early Thoughts

How many people do you know that can be said to have wisdom or who are wise in some way? Most probably none or maybe one, as with few exceptions the majority do not have particularly wise relatives or friends. The vast majority of humankind does not, and will not ever have the time, money, or the determination to search for any kind of wisdom. The general population obtains much of its knowledge from the media, newspapers, television, advertising, and movies. While there are many self-help articles and books available, they are far from and certainly lack anything remotely akin to wisdom.

A general definition of wisdom is "having the insight and judgment of how to best use one's knowledge." The Greek philosophers Socrates and Plato thought that one should love wisdom, which is where the word philosophy comes from as philo, (love) and sophia, (wisdom). Aristotle, another Greek philosopher, thought that wisdom was the ability to comprehend the causes of how things got to be the way they are. Similarly, Buddha taught a practice of meditation that leads to wisdom as "deeper insights into how things are."

The human condition is that most live as if in a mist, or the mystery of existence. Most religious writings and teachings consist of only allegories of reality that are culturally biased. In other words, various human groups have, through time, developed stories to reveal the metaphysical origin of existence, and each story is relevant only to specific cultural ways of comprehending reality. Consequently, people attend the popular services of these religions but the reality is that they are just going through repetitive rituals that at best are comforting and inspiring.

Hymns may be sung, and the individual can listen to an inspiring sermon, and give an offering to support the good works of the religion. Religious rituals also serve as a social experience of meeting others and promoting fellowship. The individual does not really learn anything about what religion has clumsily sought to reveal.

Religious ritual behaviors and socializing is at the kindergarten level, and attention is directed only to the surface reality of appearance producing a lack of depth and meaningful comprehension. It is not possible to experience metaphysical depths of comprehension but can be achieved only by observing and exploring within oneself. Through hundreds of books I have explored many ideas, but all of these books are just letters and syllabic word and alphabetic letter squiggles on paper. Each individual must be an explorer and not fall asleep in the comforting yet confining routines of life. Each individual should be an explorer of the energy depths of body and consciousness. Studying the human condition through history, it can easily be determined that neither disease, nor natural disasters, nor governments, nor religions are the major causes of suffering for humankind, but that strife can be traced to the failure of self exploration.

The body is a mystery of function. It is easily forgotten by adults how as a child, seeing, hearing, smelling, tasting, and touching, is somewhat of a small miracle. I recall in biology class watching slides of how a cell divides, and for quite a while afterward straining to comprehend how it can possibly happen. These functions of the body were mysteries that I later explored in adulthood. For example, in the study of life extension, the upper limit of the human life span is one-hundred-twenty years. To live a healthy life, it should be mandatory that each individual learn about the body, about how each part functions.

Each individual can learn to take vitamins and minerals and eat nutritious organic food that is not contaminated with pesticides, herbicides, antibiotics, or hormones. Each can keep fit through exercise like walking, lifting light weights, and practicing yoga, and each is able to obtain basic blood tests to determine what is going on unseen with cholesterol, glucose, and insulin levels.

The mind function of the brain is a mystery to be explored. As many philosophical disciplines have found, the way par excellence to explore one's mental and physical life is through introspective meditation. In one way or another, the practice of meditation seeks to direct attention from its habitual outer direction to inward psychological processes. With attention directed inward, aesthetic sensitivity to and awareness of physical and cognitive functions can be developed.

While most times analogies are not accurate, the use of one will at least get the basic point across. I compare the human body to the mechanism of a projector, the older mechanical kind with a slide tray that today is digital. Slowly over time, the idea for a projector was developed and eventually earth materials were assembled to make the parts that eventually became a projector. Now, does this mean that there is a personal maker who had the idea, and through volition made humans, like the projector was made? My response to this question is that the non-living and living forms of existence did not come from an intellect or mind, and so are not derived from thoughts or ideas like an artifact. There is an enormous reality gulf of difference between organic life forms and mechanical or electronic contrivances. But at least similar to the human body, the projector consists of parts, and for the living human body and the non-living projector, the existent parts of both have to function properly to be useful.

As self-conscious awareness is vital for human function, so a vital part of the projector is the light bulb. The projector could work, but without the light emanating from the bulb, no images would be projected. Now human conscious awareness is associated with what we call the mind, a referent literally meaning "my in." The conscious awareness of humans I equate with the light bulb.

The display of images in humans occurs when sensations from the senses are organized into images, when awake or when dreaming, by what is called the mind function of the brain. This is roughly similar to the way a slide or digital image enters the light of the projector and is projected.

The mind function of the brain transforms sensations from the senses into images and arranges them as time-slides of past memory, present, and future imagination which are propelled by volition and emotion occurring in the body. Unlike the projector, humans have to be responsible for the images they project, of how one sees past, present, and future behaviors.

The energy for the running of, and the light of the projector, comes from electricity which is produced by a generator located at a distance and is usually unseen by users. Likewise, there is a cosmic generator which generates the energy of elements, the light of stars and suns, the reflected light of moons and comets, and the light of consciousness of living forms. Now, where did this ultimate super generator come from, and just where is it located? In the past and even today, it is thought by theologians and popular thinking that a human-like god was the generator of existence. However, there is no evidence whatsoever of a human-like god. Personally I've always liked the words of the Greek philosopher Xenophanes (circa 570-475 BCE) who said, "Humans create the gods in their own image. But if cattle and horses or lions had hands, or were able to draw with their hands and do the work that human men can do, horses would draw the forms of the gods like horses, and cattle like cattle, and they would make their bodies such as they each had themselves." While Xenophanes refers to the sculpted Greek gods, the statement is also true of the invisible god of Judaism, Christianity, and Islam. It cannot be otherwise as all gods have to be portrayed as having a human-like personality.

The science of modern physics says that what appears to be empty space is actually a field that is generating the space-time continuum of relative reality. A speculative theory known as M Theory says that in an eleventh dimension there exist "membranes or branes" which eventually collide and explode to cause the Big Bang of the visible universe.

In this view there have been many Big Bangs, and therefore many universes in the past, many universes in the present, and there will be many universes in the future. The Super String theory explains that the impact fragments of the membranes became what are known as the theoretical particles of "super strings."

These are said to be a billion, billion times smaller than atoms and make up all relative things, and which exist in nine dimensions and one of time for a total of ten dimensions. These theories of the science of physics are of course all theoretical, as they will most likely never be observed or tested, so cannot be accepted as empirical science. But they do exist as monumental attempts to inferentially explain what the generator of existence is.

In regard to religion and science, the most that can be said is that there are differing metaphors for some sort of generator out there which in the past, present, and future, has, does, and will continue to generate all inanimate and animate formations. From the view of a short human lifespan, the generator is eternal, and always existing to function. There is a generator and a direct continuum of generating ever present in the vastness of space, the natural environment of the earth, and the generating within during the reproduction of all life forms. The originating cosmic force is both the generator and the terminator of existence.

All things are generated to exist as phenomena for a time, time essentially meaning continuing to be tied to the generating source as relative forms. Termination of relative existence is not a return to a relative nothing, but a return to the cosmic generator. Beyond this, speculation degenerates into imagination, as there is a surplus of stories on the topic of what exists beyond relative sensory physical reality. The ancient litany of religion is replete with heavens, purgatories, and hells, and even the modern Super String Theory speaks of other unverified dimensions. Some are convinced that the generator of existence is eternal, and that the generation of humans is special, that humans are also eternal, and after death continue to exist in another dimension.

But this way of thinking begs a question, "Why does the generator generate?" and if there is some remnant of the individual that exists after death, "Might it continue as the non-coherent random energy of nature or in some coherent spiritual way?"

Since these questions pertain to what is transcendent of human experience, it is not possible to answer why the cosmic generator generates and then terminates the forms it brings forth.

The process can only be observed. Based on experience, it is at least possible the force and energy that make up human beings continues in a coherent form. But each is convinced only by experience, so silence on this topic is usually the best policy.

Chapter 3

*Pretty much all the honest truth-telling there is in the world is done by children. Oliver Wendell Holmes*

God Maker

Benjamin Franklin (1706-1790) is credited with having first formulated the definition that "man is a tool-making animal." Until recently, humans have been defined as the only tool-maker and tool-user species. Recently evidence has been accumulated to show that chimpanzees, orangutans, gorillas, macaques, crows, dolphins, elephants, sea otters, octopuses, and Galapagos Island finches, also make and use tools. Since these mentioned species, and more, make and/or use tools, a new definition of "what it is to be human" is needed. What really defines and sets humans apart from all other living species is that they make gods. No other tool-making and tool-using species has been known to fashion gods. Of all living species, only humans are god makers.

Childhood Egoism and Animism

The making of a human-like god and origin of religion and can be found in the innate cognitive processes of children. Jean Piaget (1896-1980) was a Swiss researcher who observed evidence of four sequential stages of cognitive development in children. Piaget referred to study of these progressive biological stages of cognitive development as "genetic epistemology," meaning, biological stages of acquiring knowledge. The developmental stage and approximate age are as follows:

Sensorimotor – birth to two years
Preoperational - two to seven years
Concrete Operations – seven to eleven years
Formal Operations - eleven to twelve years

In the sensorimotor stage, from birth to two years of age, the child is concerned with bodily movement and sensing and learning about physical objects. In the preoperational stage, from two to seven years of age, the child is occupied with developing verbal skills. In the concrete operations stage, from seven to eleven years of age, the child develops the ability to use reasoning including the use of numbers and relationships. In the formal operations stage, occurring around eleven or twelve years of age, the child begins to reason logically.

During the sensorimotor stage, a phenomenon occurs known as "object permanence" or object constancy. It is at this stage that the developing child's mind/brain begins to organize sensations into memory formations, so that when an object is not immediately present to the senses, the child knows that it continues to exist. Prior to this stage, when an object is shown to the child and then removed from sight, he or she does not search for it. It has been suggested that for the child, the object exists only when seen and when not seen the object no longer exists. At the onset of object permanence, the child will actively search for an object when it is removed from sight, as the child "knows" or comprehends that the object continues to exist even when not present to the senses. Objects, including the child's own body, are remembered as stable enduring formations. More recent empirical study supports Piaget's view, and has found convincing evidence that suggests object permanence exists in infants as early as fourteen months of age.

Empirical study suggests that ego construction or a sense of self occurs within the developing child beginning with object permanence. The developing mental ability of thought, memory, and imagination begin to become more prominent through increasing sensate experience. This stabilizing of reality experience through an increase in the ability for thought, memory, and imagination, is the beginning of the formation of a stable self or ego. Piaget states, children have an "innate egocentricity." For the developing child, identification of self and others consists of a focus on physical form rather than mental processes. Only later when reaching the formal operations stage, do children have the ability, become more aware of, and begin to identify with mental processes as the self.

## Childhood Participation

Piaget defines the term "participation" as a relation that the immature thought of a child perceives to "exist between two beings or two phenomena which it regards either as partially identical or as having a direct influence on one another, although there is no spatial contact or intelligible causal connection between them." Views of participation or relationship arise when the child begins to differentiate between his or her physical body and the external environment. Through experience the child eventually detects differences between his or her physical self and the environment. There is a perceived relationship with the motion and change of the animate and inanimate environment. For a child, the functions of the environment are a "social organization."

The child perceives the environment to be related with human experience, as human-like. The child's comprehension of the relation and participation between humans and the inanimate environment consist of three dynamics:

Humans control or influence the environment.
Environmental forms are animate or alive.
Humans and the environment respond to each other and share a social relationship.

Since humans are central to and control events in the life of the child, the adults are perceived to control and influence the inanimate environment. The child observes the adults arranging the home environment and extends this to the greater natural environment and movements of the wind, water, sun, and moon. The child eventually begins to equate, identify, and see the movement and functions of the environment as equal to, and as alive as humans and animals. Since the environmental forms move, they are perceived as alive. Therefore, the change of the sun and moon is a response of what is living. For example, a child explains that the clouds grow bigger, "because we grow bigger."

Things are related to and behave as humans do. A child also explains that the moon grows bigger "because we grow bigger" and that the moon is alive "because we are alive."

Children invent or see participations by using themselves as a model or standard; the cause of the moon growing is that humans grow. This view occurs as the result of learning that he or she is growing and/or will grow big someday. The natural formations of the environment participate with humans, and respond to human needs. The sun shines for humans to have light. The shining of the sun or moon is seen as a behavior of a living presence.

Piaget further observed that the cognitive function of participation is primary and is soon followed by animism, or the perception that things in the environment that move and change are alive. Piaget states that "the notion of participation leads to that of animism and by nature precedes it." When the child is questioned about his or her ideas of participation, the child usually offers animistic explanations. Piaget sees, and I agree, that the innate ability for comparison is the origin of animism, and that the perception that things in the environment that move and change are alive as the child is alive. For example, when asked if a cloud or a stream "knows" or "feels" that it is moving, the child replies yes. When asked if humans "make" the clouds grow bigger, the child replies, "No, it isn't us, but the clouds know we are growing." This answer implies that the clouds are alive, observe, have knowledge, and grow as humans do. The perception that the formations of the environment have intentions and thoughts is anthropomorphism.

Childhood Animism

Piaget observed that beginning in the preoperational and extending through to the formal operations stage, children innately exhibit animistic thinking. Piaget defined childhood animism as the "tendency to regard objects as living and endowed with will." Modern psychology defines animism as "the attribution of life to nonliving forms." However, it can be argued that seeing things as alive and as having thoughts are separate and distinct perceptual processes. In my view, perception of nonliving forms to be alive would be animism, while the attribution of thoughts or intention would be anthropomorphism, defined as, "the attribution of human qualities to nonhuman things and events."

Perception is defined as "a subconscious cognitive process to find significance or meaning." This is in contrast to conception, which is a "conscious cognitive process of reason to find significance or meaning."

Piaget thinks the phenomena of animism is innate, occurs developmentally and "results from egocentricity" of not accurately distinguishing between mental processes of the self and events in the environment. From approximately two to eleven years of age, children exhibit the innate tendency to perceive and attribute life and "consciousness" to objects that Piaget defined as the ability to feel and know. This occurs in four overlapping stages.

If anything is active, even if stationary.
Is restricted only to what moves.
Only if movement occurs on its own, and not by an outside force.
Finally, only to animals and plants.

Piaget claims to have observed evidence of animistic thinking in children as early as twenty months. My explanation for animism is that the child experiences the motion of his or her own body, observes the movement of parents, family members, and perhaps animal or pets, and so attributes and assumes that anything that moves must be alive and have volition.

As the child becomes more aware and familiar with rudimentary thought and intentions as exhibited in the movement of his or her body, and the response movements of parents and family, the child attributes thoughts and willing intentions to all animate and inanimate forms. Whatever moves "is alive" and based on the child's own experience, the origin of that movement is thought and willed intention. When questioned, young children define "alive" as the ability "to do something ... to be able to move." For the child there is no distinction of internal and external intention. The child interacts with living forms, his or her own parents and other humans and perhaps animal or pets.

Eventually in the sensorimotor stage the child learns or becomes aware that intention is related to bodily movement, and that adult's move to gratify one's desires.

This schema or pattern is imposed on the environment, so that any movement is perceived to occur through the willful intention of a living form.

Childhood Artificialism

Piaget observed that during the early developing stage of artificialism, when asked what an object is, (for example a fork,) the child replies that "it is for eating." A lake is said to be for "going on with a boat," or "for fishes," or "for swimming in." There is a focus on present function and none on the past origin of the object. Eventually the child is then observed to answer in response to what an object is, that it was "made for" a certain function.

The child observes the parents preparing and bringing food, and the giving of objects to play with. The parents are then spontaneously viewed as the "makers of things." All things are seen as coming from the parents, and that they are the "origin of, or makers" of the child and all objects including the environment. Piaget observed that between four and seven years of age, children first develop a curiosity and interest in his or her birth, and where he or she came from. They then progress to wanting to know the origin of the first human, or all humans. Lastly they ask questions about the origin of all things, including the environment. Questions in regard to some primal or ultimate cause, such as, "who or what made everything," begin to be asked at about six to seven years of age.

A child begins to investigate its origin by asking questions of "where" it was before birth. This is a concern with a spatial rather than a causal origin. The child then progresses to the next stage of questioning and asks and wants to know how babies are "made." The child spontaneously associates this activity with the parents. Piaget defines "artificialism" as "the child's tendency to explain the origin of things as having been made by humans." The child begins to think of "where things have come from" in terms of "artifice" or things made.

Between two and three years of age, children spontaneously begin to ask artificer questions such as, "Who made the sun?"

The natural environment is perceived or comprehended as an "artifact," a product of human activity and being handmade in some way. According to Piaget's findings, the artificer or maker is first thought of to be one's parents, and this is later attributed to human workers in general.

Piaget distinguishes sequential overlapping stages in the development of artificialism. The first two stages develop between three and seven years of age. The first stage is "diffuse artificialism," which has a basis in the child's material dependence upon his or her parents and where the child observes adult behaviors. The next stage is "mythological artificialism," which is the tendency, when questioned regarding the origin of things, to spontaneously construct short stories of how things were made by humans. An example would be "the sun was made from a stone or match, and the sky, night, mountains and rivers, were all made by humans." It is interesting to note during this time, that the processes of animism and artificialism continue to complement one another, as things are "alive" and "made" at the same time.

The stage of "technical artificialism" develops at about the age of seven. At this time, the environment is perceived to function on its own, and causal relationships are recognized. Through a combination of influences including observation, social interaction, and education, the child begins to comprehend things and events. The child also questions how things work or function in terms of interrelated natural processes of the environment. Finally during the ages of nine to ten years, the onset of "immanent artificialism" occurs. This is the stage when the view that "the environment is made by humans" fades. Eventually at ten to eleven years of age, children develop the view that the environment has a "natural origin." with the gradual recognition that humans are dependent upon, and subject to, the processes of nature. It is then that the cognitive process of animism, and artificialism gradually decline.

During the process of maturation, children find out the limited capacity of parents and humans, and then after being introduced to religious teachings, accept religious views.

When children are questioned, they explain that all things come from "a god." The overwhelming evidence is these childhood perceptual and conceptual processes do not completely disappear upon reaching early adulthood. Childhood artificialism is the precursor to what is known later as anthropomorphism in the adult, and which contributes to the development of religion. I define anthropomorphism as "the attribution of human qualities to nonhuman things and events." All later anthropomorphic religions are but the continuation of childhood participation, animistic and artificer thinking. The cognitive immaturity of the child continues in the cognitively immature adult. These innate cognitive processes observed in children are also observed in the cognitive processes of adults. In children, animistic and artificer thinking attributes thoughts and intentions to moving environmental processes. Likewise, many adults are convinced that the origin of environmental forms are the effect of the human-like thoughts of a god. The adult then utilizes faith (Latin word "fidere," or "trust") to affirm that there is a human-like protective presence of a god.

Animism and artificialism are anthropocentric, pre-causal ways of explaining things and events. In animism, inanimate forms such as the sun, moon, wind, and water, are alive and have intentions. At this stage the child explains objects in terms of function and utility. For example, when asked, "What is the sun?" the child replies that the sun is "for" light or warmth, the clouds are "for" making rain. With the onset of artificialism, the intentions belong to the makers of things and events, which are the parents and humans. When asked, "What is the sun or water?" the child replies, the sun is "made for" warmth or light and water is "made for" drinking.

Children want to know where they were before they were born. They usually question where the parents found, bought, or obtained the child. They think of themselves as preexisting and alive in some way. As a result of dependence on parents, they develop questions of how they were made by the parents. The parents become a causal explanation. This is artificialism. The child thinks of him or herself as being assembled from parts by the parents or having come from the parent's body.

Eventually the child questions where humans came from, and at age six to seven, the child questions the presence of some primal or first beginning.

From ages of seven to ten years, children begin to evidence a decrease of egocentric and anthropocentric views and increasingly seek to comprehend the physical determinism of natural processes. Based on the experience of dependence on the parents, and his or her spontaneous veneration of them, and when encountering adult religious teachings, these feelings are then transferred to an anthropomorphized adult god. This god then functions as a primal human-like ancestor and the cause of humans and the environment. Piaget states that the child's idea of a god is that of a "greater human."

Piaget distinguishes four evolving stages of reality in the transition from childhood rudimentary awareness of thinking to a more mature awareness of mental processes.

Absolute realism.
Immediate realism.
Mediate realism.
Subjectivism or relativism.

For the child in the first stage of absolute realism, there is a lack of awareness of mental processes of thought occurring within, and only physical bodies, including the child's body and objects, are real. The child considers the reality of all existence as mainly physical. The child progresses through the immediate stage, and the mediate stages, to the subjectivism or relativism stage. This is when the child becomes more aware of the immaterial mental processes of thought occurring within him or herself.

Piaget observed that in the early stages of childhood, only what is "external" is real to the child, and that there is no ability for introspection. For Piaget, it is "ignorance" of his or her own mental processes which leads a child to animistically attribute life and volition to nonliving things. Piaget says, "The fact is that the less a mind is given to introspection the more it is the victim of illusion that it knows itself perfectly."

"We all know that we have illusions concerning ourselves and that knowledge of one's self is the hardest of all knowledge. Of this, a mind uncultivated, like the child's, knows nothing." Piaget further remarks, "In short, for a mind that cannot distinguish, or does so but dimly, the self [mental processes] from the external world, everything participates in the nature of and can influence everything else."

Piaget's view here is that introspection does not occur naturally in children or adults, and that for the child, the self or ego is the physical body. The child's attention is not focused on the "internal and subjective act of thinking" and therefore there is "an absence of differentiation between the self (or thought) and the external world." As the child cognitively matures, there is a 'growth of self-consciousness" and therefore a progressive "depersonalization" of objective reality of the environment occurs. What Piaget means by depersonalization, is that the child ceases to animistically attribute aliveness, consciousness, and human-like intention to the environment.

The perceptual ability to distinguish between internal and external, and mental and material occurs at about eleven years of age. Prior to this age, the child has not fully developed the ability or learned to distinguish his or herself from external things, and so does not distinguish the subjective from the objective. The main focus of attention of the child is on physical forms that probably occurs as a result of satisfying needs in the environment.

Piaget has admirably discussed the cognitive developmental of human god-making in children but there also exist other adult subconscious and conscious processes and motivations as well. Comments and brief quotes by Jean Piaget have been taken from various editions of his profoundly insightful book, *The Child's Conception of the World*.

Adult Animism

Modern psychology provides a definition of animism as "the attribution of life to nonliving forms." Animism is an innate and early developed cognitive function of the perceptual system that is oriented to changes in motion and to relationships. The human brain/mind interprets these changes as caused by internal or external factors. Concepts of aliveness, intent, and purpose are based upon this primitive biological function. For early humans, the movement of a comet, an avalanche, or a thunderstorm behaved as an intentional, living entity.

Early human experience that life comes from life and not from what was dead or unmoving. The observation of plants and trees growing from the soil and insects and animals entering and exiting holes and dens probably resulted in the animistic view that the earth was alive. Animism is a contributing factor to the development of religion, as early humans perceived moving processes as living and then projected onto them mental processes of intentions and thoughts. Early or prehistoric peoples attributed the processes of the environment to an animating entity having intentional thoughts. Not utilizing cause and effect to explain the motion or function of natural processes, humans used what they were most familiar with in their own evolving self-awareness. The movement of flowing water, storms, sun, moon, and planets were comprehended as being alive and as having conscious thoughts. For early humans, any natural phenomenon that moved was perceived as an animated entity capable of thinking and willful intending. This cognitive process of attributing thoughts to natural and supernatural forms is known as anthropomorphism.

The perceptual processes of animism and anthropomorphism are complimentary. Attributing aliveness is animism while attributing thought and willing intention is anthropomorphism. Animism and anthropomorphism are perceptual processes (innate and subconscious) and border on conscious analogy. The child perceives all moving and changing things to be alive like he is or his living parents. The moving perceived living things also have intentions and thoughts like him or his parents.

Analogy is also a conceptual process, and the result of conscious thinking and reasoning "that is like this."

The child eventually becomes aware that thought precedes or accompanies movement of the body. Using the self as analogy, then other things that move must also be alive and have thoughts and intentions. Children spontaneously use analogy which they confuse with causality. This is also true of religion oriented adults who confuse subconscious and conscious modes of analogical thought with causality.

Anthropomorphism

The origin of religion has come about through the psychological process of perception known as anthropomorphism. Anthropomorphism is a rudimentary and cognitively immature way of comprehending cause and effect processes. It is the expression of a first and feeble metaphysical yearning to comprehend the origin of the environment, life, and the ending of things. In early times, to recognize the origin of the environment and of life, humans' projected personal qualities such as intentions, caring, love, and protection onto visible god and goddess figures. Later these same qualities were projected to unseen human-like gods. The perceptual process of anthropomorphism in humans contributed to the origin and development of religion. Anthropomorphism is a result of an evolving yet cognitive immaturity, prejudiced in favor of humans, confirmed by the religious group, as a result of the experience of mental and physical personal limitation within, and in the environment.

A view favoring anthropomorphism as contributing to the development of religion is that of Sigmund Freud (1865-1939) who defined religion as "a psychological delusion, a mistaken idea." For Freud, the phenomena of both a cooperative civilization and religious views originated from the need to defend oneself against the superior forces of nature. This is done by humanizing nature, since impersonal forces cannot be communicated with by humans. By attributing a human-like volition or will to the forces of nature, humans seek to influence nature. This cognitive process originates in the phylogenetic and individual helplessness of childhood that gives the attributes of a father to environmental forces.

Freud thought that having a god is a wish-fulfilling illusion or delusion. Religion has its beginnings in emotion, phylogenetic instinct, and subconscious childhood memories. Religion is not the result of intelligent reasoning processes, but is the cognitive distortion of an obsessional neurosis.

In contrast, my view of the cognitive origin and development of religion is based on the earliest use and meaning of the word, which is to find one's way back to or to make the unknown source of life and the environment known. Religion is not only a projection, it is also a cognitive strategy to determine the beginning or origin of existence and events. I do agree with Freud that forces of the environment have been humanized or anthropomorphized. While Freud implies the cognitive function of animism, of attributing life to non-living forms, he does not specifically mention it in his view. I also agree with Freud that anthropomorphism is a subconscious cognitive process that aids in human survival strategy, and that it is a mistaken idea. While humans can anthropomorphically obsess about the origin of existence, I would not consider this to be a neurosis or cognitive dysfunction but rather a way of surviving the difficulties of existence. Freud attributes the mechanism of anthropomorphism to phylogenetic instinct, which I also comprehend to be innate. I accept Freud's view of anthropomorphism as an innate cognitive process, and I also accept that the subconscious memories of childhood contribute to the phenomenon of anthropomorphism and the beginning of religion.

The most basic expression of religion originates in subconscious perception using human attributes. A number of recent studies suggest the cognitive tendency to anthropomorphism is innate. Research with newborn and older infants has found that sub-cortical or innate mechanisms predispose newborns to look toward a human face, rather than other stimuli. Also, results measured at six and twelve week intervals suggest an increase in cortical influence over infant preference to respond to the human face.

Studies show an innate predisposition to seek and cognize human features in the environment that contribute to the later perceptual mechanism of anthropomorphism.

If the origin of existence was not human-like the origin of existence and events could not have been identified. Without a human-like beginning there would have been no possible way to identify the origin or cause of existence. Socially there would have been no model of authority or standard to follow for the culture. Without a human-like model there would be no higher civil life as contrasted with the lower standards of life. There would be little progress in the establishing of standards and of separating what is good from what is bad, evil or disliked. A god serves as a model guide for behavior, of what is right or wrong, good or bad. An ethical based religion attempts to define how to become a good or higher god-like person versus how not to be a bad or evil lower devil-like person. Not having one higher god above, there could have been no way to enforce social order below. Having one god is a symbol of one origin, of one force, also symbolizing a single volition to do what is wanted by religious and political leaders. A god who punishes, also sanctions punishment by an earthly authority. Without one authority there would be conflicting and opposing views. God also serves as a model of one authority to unite and obey during aggression with opposing countries or cultures. It is a comfort to many adults that the source of the environment and life has thoughts like humans so it can be communicated with.

Analogical Reasoning

While Freud thought that religion began in genetic instinct and subconscious memory, and emotions of fear and helplessness experienced during childhood, he did not think that conscious reasoning was an influence. In my view, rudimentary reasoning using analogy, comparing "this with that," is a cognitive process that has greatly contributed to the origin and development of religion.

Along with the cognitive processes of animism, artificialism and anthropomorphism, evidence suggests that rudimentary reasoning using analogy also influenced the development of religion.

It is evident that the conscious use of analogy has also contributed to the origin of religion in the written record of humankind, as humans using reason created gods and goddess in their own image.

From earliest times and from every culture, came imaginatively reasoned myths, stories of gods and goddesses, whether visible or invisible, many or one. Still, the same process of anthropomorphism is at work here. Over time it was realized gods and goddesses never appeared to anyone, just in stories, and a gradual refinement began to occur. Many gods and goddesses were eventually refined to one, which was invisible, yet retained a personality.

As recorded throughout historic times, there have been thousands of gods and goddesses, particular to many human cultures. This phenomenon begs a question, "Are all of these many deities real, and have these cultures been correct in their faith in these deities?" One explanation is that all of the worshipped gods and goddesses are real and existing, or that only certain ones of these gods and goddesses actually exist. Another explanation is that there is only one true god out of all of them, and the rest are false. Which is which? The most probable and truthful explanation for the plurality of gods is not that they actually exist, but rather that there exists in humans certain cognitive processes responsible for all of the many deities.

In conclusion, there are three cognitive processes which in combination serve to construct the religious view of a god. These are animism, anthropomorphism, and analogical reasoning. Beginning in childhood and continuing into adulthood, the environment is perceived to be the result of a willful intention. The developed practice of a reconnection process, known as religion, is an attempt to reconnect with that which moves all of existence. The dynamic for this occurs through the knowing processes of animism and anthropomorphism, which are affirmed by analogical reasoning; there must be a human-like presence which all has come from.

Edward Conklin

Chapter 4

*In all things of nature there is something of the miraculous. Aristotle*

Prehistoric and Historic Beginnings

The English word religion is traced to the Latin word *ligare,* meaning, to connect, and the prefix *re*, meaning, again. The word religion literally means to "connect again" to what brings all things into existence and causes events to occur. The primary intention of religion has been, and continues to be an attempt to comprehend and relate with the origin of the environment and life. By means of religion, humans have always sought to know from where or what all things, including themselves, have come from. They also want to know to what or where all things will go at the time of physical death.

When did humans develop a religious view? Humans became religious when, during the course of evolution, the innate ability for animistic perception developed to see nonliving events in the environment as alive. Religion developed further when humans began to express the innate ability for anthropomorphism, and to perceive and posit human attributes to nonhuman things and events.

The innate evolved ability for animistic and anthropomorphic perception surely had a long period of development. Eventually perceptual and evolved conceptual ability for rudimentary reasoning began to be expressed in behaviors. While there is no actual evidence for religious thoughts, there are behavioral artifacts which suggest specific cognitive processes of religious thinking. When did these innate perceptual and conceptual abilities begin to be expressed and to develop into a religion or religious view? Evidence suggests that religion began with the species of humans known as Neanderthals. Religion first began in the Paleolithic Age and continued to be developed through modern times to include the many gods and goddesses over all the lands of the earth.

The evidence suggests that circa 100,000 to 10,000 years ago, early humans cognitively located the origin of existence in the environment through identifying attributes that resembled the human female. In prehistoric times, the earth was perceived and conceived to be a greater mother from which life came into existence. While many would be hesitant to seek the presence of religion so long ago, based on artifact remains, there is evidence of religious thinking and behavior that suggests a concern by early humans for the origin of existence. The three artifact areas of evidence are Neanderthal burial, European Paleolithic cave art and female figurines. These artifacts, more than any other early endeavor, reveal the human comprehension that the beginning of all life came from within the earth, including plant, animal, and human existence.

What eventually developed was a long lasting geocentric (earth-centered) and gynocentric (female-centered) religious view. Numerous research views exist regarding the phenomena of human burials that began with Neanderthals circa 100,000 BCE, and continued until the extinction of the line circa 30,000 BCE. Some of these include the view that the burials were not intentional, whereas others are convinced that the burials were intentional. When intentional, views vary as to the intention, they range from emotional bonds, to hygiene, and accidental burial. Those who argue that the burials were not intentional ignore convincing evidence of intentional burial, while views for intentional interment lack grounding in the artifact evidence, and often rely on the use of analogy with contemporary tribal cultures.

The evidence strongly suggests that Neanderthal burials were intentional, and this interaction with the earth indicates a geocentric religious view. The interring of the human body in the soil beneath rock-shelters and in caves reveals the strategic view that the origin of life came from within the earth. Neanderthals, having a brain similar to modern humans, had the cognitive capacity for two mostly subconscious, as well as conscious, mental processes. The first is animism, or attributing life to non-living things, and the second is anthropomorphism, the mostly subconscious attribution of human characteristics to nonhuman things or processes.

A Neanderthal ability to think and reason is evident in subsistence patterns that suggest planning and the imitative making of sixty-three kinds of flake tools and twenty-one variations of the hand axe. This implies that they were also capable of the conscious process of rudimentary analogical reasoning; in other words, they could have reasoned simply "this is like that." Both Neanderthal genders, through the cognitive processes of animism, anthropomorphism, and analogical reasoning, were the first humans to perceive and liken or gynocentrically compare a physical birth to their group origin from the cave openings and the interior of the earth. In this way, Neanderthals introduced the earliest and first religion of humankind.

Evidence of this religious conception of the interior of the earth as the origin of life continued with Homo sapiens sapiens from the beginnings of European cave art circa 35,000 BCE until the end of this artistic behavior circa 10,000 BCE. Numerous theories attempt to explain the existence of Paleolithic parietal art, which is defined as images engraved, drawn, painted, or sculpted on the ceilings, walls, and floors of caves. The most popular view of researchers is that the cave art was made exclusively by males as an expression of hunting, fertility magic, and shamanistic rituals. However, research has shown that less than four percent of the animal depictions have marks on them that could be interpreted as weapons, and the images are never portrayed alarmed as a result of being wounded. The fertility magic and shamanistic theories are not convincingly supported by relevant artifact remains, and are often speculative, and rely on the use of analogy with historic tribal groups.

The images of animals, plants, and human hand prints were drawn primarily by women as a result of the perceptual processes of animism, anthropomorphism, dream imagery, and the analogically reasoned gynocentric view that the interior of the earth was the female-like greater origin of life. Therefore, the cave art images were a "petition" by the artists, who acted as "midwives" in assisting the earth to bring forth the portrayed living forms.

Just as women made life within the interior of their abdomen and eventually gave birth, so they gathered within the greater interior of caves to petition and assist the earth to bring to life the various animals, by engraving and painting likenesses of these living forms.

Archeological support for this view is also found in the prevalence of smaller hand prints and footprints left by the artists in a number of caves in France and Spain. This petitionary-midwife model also explains an important anomaly in the faunal record, for which few previous explanations have been offered or are convincing, regarding the discrepancy between the species of animals depicted in the cave art, and the remains of the animals eaten by the inhabitants. The bones of the animals portrayed most often are not frequently found, while the bones of the animals not portrayed are found in great quantity. An explanation for this phenomenon is that the makers of the art are petitioning for the animals that they want and do not have.

The third area of evidence of a Paleolithic religion is that of the female "Venus" figures produced from circa 30,000-12,000 BCE. Theories for this phenomenon of sculpted and engraved human female images range from the view that they functioned as figures to increase or glorify human fertility, or reproduction, as a recognition or honoring womanhood. My findings show that these views are not convincingly supported by the artifact remains, and that they rely exclusively on research obtained from, or associated with modern women.

The Venus figures have few facial features, the feet are missing, and the hands are often not present. While marked on the Willendorf Venus and a few others, the vulvae are missing from the majority of images, nipples are not indicated on the breasts, and the Venus figures are never depicted in childbirth, nursing newborns, or with children. Moreover, there is little evidence of clothing. These characteristics strongly prompt a question. Are these Venus figures an accurate image of the human female? The answer would have to be no. The artists omitted the details that would have represented women naturalistically.

Lacking these details, which the artists seem quite capable of representing, the Venus figures are generalized images of the human body and are not particularly identifiable females. In my view, these female figurines are not Venus figures, but are rather "Earth" figures.

They are the earliest anthropomorphism of a deity, namely the interior of the earth as the female origin of human, animal, and plant life. The unknown shape of the earth was made known through anthropomorphizing it. The figures are a conceived gynocentric and geocentric combination and expression of the knowledge early humans had, of where life originated, the human female body and the mysterious interior of the earth.

There was a relatively rapid decline and demise of the view that the interior of the earth was the origin of life, which is evident in the cessation of the making of the cave art animal and plant images, and the female figures circa 10,000 BCE. Some of the events that contributed to the collapse of the long term geocentric and gynocentric religious view of the Paleolithic people include a changing environment, domestication of animals and plants, and most importantly, the eventual awareness of the male role in the process of reproduction. This comprehension of the male contribution to reproduction is evident in the increasing presence of anthropocentrism and androcentrism in the content of Late Paleolithic and early Neolithic art. Excavations near a town in eastern Germany have revealed the earliest Neolithic male statue. The 7,200 year old clay statue figure was given the name Adonis of Zschernitz. The lower half of the torso, hips, and upper thighs remain of the original eight inch high clay statue, and distinctly display what remains of a broken penis and testicles. There are also markings on the body that might represent tattoos.

Egoism

Ego is the Latin term for "the human sense of personality, of self, of what an individual thinks they are." During childhood and adulthood, constructing an ego inside has advantages and the benefits of a stable self-identity.

However, in ego development there can be too much of a good thing, or not enough of a good thing so that having an ego is often a problem. There is a saying in mental health that "neurotics build sand castles in the air, psychotics live in them, and psychiatrists/psychologists collect the rent."

The term "shrink" or "headshrinker" refers to the task of a therapist who, during the course of psychotherapy, seeks to shrink or reduce the over importance an individual has attributed to his or her personal experience. Psychotherapy is a process of adjusting ego balance of an over-inflated or exaggerated superiority, or an inferiority. Most prevalent is an over importance, often as a way of getting attention from others or as a compensation for a sense of inferiority.

Most individuals do not seek mental health services, and consequently many suffer egotistically and needlessly. Many are embarrassed to seek mental health services, or are reluctant as they are often expensive. In America, many millions have a mental disorder in any given year, although a rough estimate is that fewer than fifteen percent seek treatment.

Giants

Conceiving of, and constructing an ego outside as a greater human-like presence has the cognitive disadvantage of not being true, while it has the advantage of providing a pre-scientific explanation of where the environment and life came from. Historically, the tales and fables of giants are probably older than the stories of gods and goddesses. Both giant and god stories are expressions of human egoism. Giants are a size and force greater than humans and are a way of explaining the cause of certain effects in the environment. While it is probable that there were occasional humans of large stature, this alone is not sufficient to explain the frequent tales of giants found in many cultures.

Giants are anthropomorphisms of the environment, which made the function of the huge natural landscape more comprehensible to early humans. Not able to comprehend unique or unusual large features of the environment to be caused by geological processes, the only way of explaining them was that they were the result of the activity of great human-like giants. The anthropomorphized image of a giant reveals both human awe and also fear of the immense size of the environment.

Giants are of flesh and blood, rough and earthy, and usually of not pleasing physical proportions. They are closely related to the earth, and so are most probably earlier conceptions than the later gods who were more refined.

Giants often lived in caves, unlike the gods or goddesses who resided in unseen spiritual dimensions. Both giants of folklore and the gods of religion are an expression of human egoism. The developmental process of a human sense of self internally, continues to be expressed externally through the popular views of giants in folklore and the gods of religion. The ego making process within the individual also constructs and projects a greater ego outside as the causal origin of the environment. This is in contrast to the cognitive process of anthropomorphism, which is the attribution of human qualities to nonhuman things and events and occurs primarily as a subconscious perceptual interpretive tendency to find significance or meaning. In contrast egoism occurs as a conscious process of conceptual reasoning. Egoism is the internal constructive act of conceiving an external super ego or self that has the human features of a giant, god or goddess.

Humans construct a self within, and also construct a greater self externally to explain their origin. While both processes are a strategy for stability within and without, both are a cognitive distortion, and a failure to accurately observe and apperceive. Within changing conditioned processes, the stable entity of a self or ego is constructed inside and outside of the individual. The outside ego is more of a survival orientation to have vicarious assistance, and to have something in control. In reality, there is no greater humanlike intelligence external to humans, only the law of cause and effect as a continuity of force and polarity of motion and momentum.

The ego of a giant or a god or goddess is only an attempt to recognize the origin of the existence of forms and events in the environment. Many cultures throughout human existence have identified the origin of existence and events through having various giants, gods, and goddesses. A few examples of giant stories are found in Greek, Nordic, Judaism, in European, and American Indian cultures.

The Greek Cyclopes (round eyes) were giants said to have a single eye in the middle of their forehead, and were said to be the children of Uranus (the sky) and Gaia (the earth). They had an irritable temperament, and were stubborn and very strong. The names of the three of them are, Arges, Brontes, and Steropes, and they are said to have made the lightning bolts for Zeus to use in defeating the Titans and his father Cronus. The Cyclopes were also the helpers of Hephaestus, the Greek god of fire, the forge, and blacksmiths. Together they forged Artemis's bow and arrows, Poseidon's trident, and the helmet Hades gave to Perseus while on his quest to kill Medusa. It is later said that when Zeus killed Apollo's son Asclepius with a lightning bolt forged by the Cyclopes, Apollo killed the Cyclopes in revenge. They are also said to have built the large stone block fortification at Mycenae, and the rumbling vent noises coming from volcanoes were said to be from their labors under the earth. The Cyclopes are a convenient way of explaining where lightning bolts come from as well as the underground crater activity of volcanoes.

In Norse tales, the primal giant Ymir spontaneously came into being from the blending of the ice region of the north, and the south region of burning coals and sparks. Other Norse giants include frost giants, fire giants, and mountain giants. Eventually the god Odin, (or Godin from which the English word god is derived) and his two brothers were born. Odin is the god of wisdom, magic, poetry, and prophecy. Odin and his brothers killed Ymir, and with his body made the earth. His blood became the waters, his bones became mountains, teeth and pieces of bones became stones, and his hair became trees. Ymir's skull became the sky and his brain the clouds. The brothers found driftwood and made the first humans, a man named Askr, associated with the ash tree, and a woman named Embla, associated with an elm tree or a vine.

There is mention of "nephilim," usually translated as "giants" in biblical mythology. Genesis 6:4 mentions, "There were giants in the earth in those days; and also after that, when the sons of God came in unto the daughters of men and they bore children to them, the same became mighty men who were of old, men of renown." This is a mistranslation, as in the Hebrew language the word nephilim (fallen ones) are not giants.

Tool-Maker to God Maker

The nephilim are said to be a people that came from the interbreeding of the "sons of the gods" (bene ha'elohim) and the "daughters of men." However, the book of Numbers 13:33 mentions the sons of Anak, who were giants. The book of Deuteronomy 2:10 mention the Emites, and the book of Joshua 12:4 mentions the Rephaites, who were giants living in the land of Cannan.

Geological features attributed to the causality of giants include stories of how huge rocks came to be found in certain locations, as the result of giants who threw boulders at one another, and who also placed large rocks in the sea near shore so that they could use them to sit on and fish. Large natural shaped rocks are also variously said to be a giant's shoe, a marble, a bowl, or a weapon. When the Giant's Causeway in Ireland first became well known by 1693, debate actually began as to whether the impressive landscape was formed by humans, nature, or the efforts of Finn MacCool, a giant who, according to legend, built the causeway to bring his lady giant love interest across the water to be with him. The Giant's Causeway is made up of forty thousand hexagon shaped stone columns, some up to forty feet high, and the tops of which seem to form stepping stones starting from the cliff base and disappearing under the seawater. Some of the stone structures also resemble objects that are said to have belonged to the giant, such as a chimney stack, harp, pipe organ, boot, and circular formations known as "the giant's eyes." It was not until the year 1771 that the Causeway's real origin was correctly attributed to volcanic eruptions, and cooling lava that occurred some fifty million years ago.

St. Michael's Mount is a rocky island about two-hundred-thirty feet above sea level, and is located about 400 yards off the coast of Cornwall England. The island is said to have been built by a giant by the name of Cormoran, who brought large granite stones to build up the island to be his home. He is also said to have waded ashore to steal cows and sheep from the residents of a nearby village. The giant was killed by a local boy who later acquired the name of "Jack the Giant Killer." There is a large pit pointed out by the locals as being the site that Jack tricked the giant into falling to his death. There is also a heart shape stone in the cobblestone walkway said to have been that of the giant.

American Indians also have giant stories. One such tale is from the Wampanong tribe who lived around the Cape Cod and Martha's Vineyard area of Massachusetts. The giant's name was Moshup, and he liked to catch whales and cook them, which required the uprooting of many trees. His need for plenty of firewood is said to be the reason so few trees grow in the area today. He also threw huge stones into the water to stand on while he caught the whales, which explains how a line of large rocks were formed along the stretch of land from Cuttyhunk to the mainland. He smoked a great pipe of tobacco, and one day emptied the ashes to form the island of Nantucket. There is also a large crater on the top of a hill near the Vineyard said to be where he liked to sit.

These are just a few examples of the ego construction of giants as a worldwide mental activity of many cultures. However, just as no remains of any tribal, Egyptian, Hindu, Greek, Roman, Hebrew god or goddess has ever been found to exist, neither have any physical remains of the great giants of legend been found. Just as the inward mental process of ego development occurs in human maturation, so the outward ego development of giants and supernatural gods and goddesses develop within human conception and imagination.

Chapter 5

*Vanity of vanities...all is vanity. Ecclesiastes 1:2*

*We created god in our own image and likeness!*
George Carlin

Judaism

Growing up in the Catskill Mountains of New York, many of my friends were Jewish. Therefore, I want to state for the record that I am not anti-Semitic but am anti-ignorance and very pro-knowledge in my endeavor to critique Jewish religious thought. Without bias then, Israel is called the "holy" land. Rather than subjectively seeing the ground area to be in some way sacred, the term can be objectively seen as the land of many bullet holes. Over the years there has been much destruction to the buildings and many of the people who reside there have been wounded or killed; just as in the past there were arrow, spear, and sword puncture holes of persons and property.

Garden of Eden

From Goli park in Tabriz, Iran, overlooking the valley of the Adji Chay river, can be seen a large cliff glowing red in the sun. The large cliff is a deposit of red ochre, a clay containing silica and iron oxides, which gives it the reddish color. Paleolithic prehistoric humans used red ochre in burials and to paint the images of animals on cave walls, which are observed in many locations in France and Spain. In the biblical Genesis story, the first human was Adam, from Hebrew "adamah," meaning, red earthling. The Genesis story mentions that Adam was formed by the god from the "dust of the earth." The Hebrew word translated as dust is "aphar," meaning, soil from which clay is made.

An amateur historian by the name of Reginald Walker (1917-1989), first proposed the theory that the Garden of Eden was located in north-west Iran. He identified the heads of the four rivers named in

Genesis 2 in the area of Tabriz, Iran. Known in English as the Garden of Eden, in Hebrew it is "Gan Eden." The word "gan" came to mean a walled or enclosed garden. The word Eden is of Sumerian origin and not Hebrew. The word refers to a plain or flat area near a village utilized for cultivation of crops and grazing of animals.

Nearing Mount Sahand, travel is through a narrow fertile valley with high mountain walls to the mud-brick town of Osku, situated on a prehistoric occupation mound. In the dark fertile soil of the mound grow olive, apple, almond and walnut trees. This very site is said to be the semi-historically remembered and imaginatively elaborated upon location of the Semitic Garden of Eden.

Another important influence of the country of Iran on the religion of Judaism occurred circa 1200 BCE, when the Iranian prophet Zoroaster introduced the concepts of a good god and an evil opposer and humankind's choice between the two. He conceived of a "sayoshant" or savior figure, a final judgment, heaven and hell, and resurrection. These key concepts are a founding influence on the later religions of Judaism, Christianity, and Islam.

## Genesis

The Garden of Eden story is the early Hebrew attempt to use a human-like model. The story explains the origin of existence, the origin of good and evil, and to establish and instill social order via the authority of a human-like god. The patriarchal religion of Judaism is based on conceiving the origin of existence to have the ego attributes of an intelligent human-like personality. The god of the bible in Genesis 3:8 was very human-like, and was said to be observed relaxing and "walking in the garden in the cool of the day." The Genesis story of the origin of existence is the imaginative and audaciously creative male attempt to replace the observed natural origin of life from female birth, and to supplant the greater origin of life from the earth as mother.

There are two distinct stories present in the Genesis tale and both were combined circa late 500's and 400's BCE, shortly after the end of the Babylonian Exile.

Genesis 1 is the northern Israelite origin story, and in this tradition the god is referred to as El or the plural gods, the Elohim. Genesis chapters 2-4 are the southern Judah story, and the god of this region was Yhwh. Brief evidence of the combining of the two stories is the use of the English phrase "the Lord God," as first used in Genesis 2:4. In Hebrew, the phrase is Yhwh Elohim, which is evidence of the combining of the two god traditions.

Genesis 1 is the northern Israelite origin story, and here the god El or gods Elohim created all things, and after each creative deed commented that, it was good.

Heaven, earth, waters, light and darkness, and it "was good"
Land and the seas and "it was good."
Grass, herbs, and fruit trees and "God saw that it was good."
Stars, sun, and moon, and these were also "good."
Animal life of the seas and whales, and the birds of the air, and this was "good."
Earthly animals including cattle and every creeping thing were also "good."
The god made humans and of this it is said was "very good"

The god blessed and spoke to the male and female, and gave them dominion over "every living thing" and "every tree." In this first story, the main points were that all things were made by the god and were good; humans were made in the god's image; animals were told to be fruitful and multiply; humans were given the fruit of every herb and every tree to eat. It is declared in Genesis 1:31, "And God saw everything he had made, and, behold, it was very good." This is an optimistic view of existence, an implied perfection and there is no mention of anything evil in this first origin story.

"And God said, Let us make man in our image, after our likeness: and let them have dominion over the fish of the sea, and over the fowl of the air, and over the cattle, and over all the earth, and over every creeping thing that creepeth upon the earth. So God created man in his own image, in the image of God created he him; male and female created he them.

And God blessed them, and God said unto them, Be fruitful, and multiply, and replenish the earth, and subdue it: and have dominion over the fish of the sea, and over the fowl of the air, and over every living thing that moveth upon the earth." (1:26-28)

The mention in Genesis 1 that male and female were created at the same time gave rise to a Jewish folklore tradition of Lilith. "So God created man in his own image, in the image of God created he him; male and female created he them." In Jewish tradition, Lilith is said to be the first wife of Adam. Only one verse in the Old Testament, that of Isaiah 34:14 mentions Lilith, but in most English translations is translated as owl or screech owl. "And there shall the beasts of the desert meet with the jackals, and the wild goat shall cry to his fellow; the lilith also shall settle there, and find for herself a place of rest." Lilith is also mentioned in a list of evil creatures in the Dead Sea Scrolls, and mentioned four times in the Talmud.

In Genesis 1, the first humans were told to go out among all other living forms and subdue them and have dominion over the earth. Later in Genesis 2, humans were willfully forced to leave the garden and then go forth upon the earth. Genesis 2 is the origin story of the southern Judah tribe of the area of Jerusalem, and the god is known as Yhwh. The first three verses of Genesis 2 are the transition from Genesis 1 into Genesis 2. In the Genesis 2 story, there is an entirely different sequence of creation.

Earth
Heavens
Plants and Herbs
Mist and water
Formed from the dust of the ground, the man Adam, which means "red earth"
Garden of Eden
Trees, pleasant and good for food
Tree of Life
Tree of Knowledge of Good and Evil
A river which also formed four other rivers
Formed from the ground beasts of the field, cattle, fowl, and subtle serpent
Formed Eve from Adam's rib

It is an old theme of humans and animals coming to life from mother earth, but here in this androcentric story the earth is not female and is lifeless. Not until the male god uses his willing, thought, and animating "ruah" meaning breath, was human life formed from the earth. While the Garden of Eden story explains how the environment, life, and humans originated, it also creates a problem. Rather than Hebrew humans observing themselves to be a related part of the greater energy movement and motion of nature, a human-like god was developed. While the god served to explain the origin of existence and to instill social order, the Genesis story also served to alienate and limit vision as a whole. By this cognitive distortion the Jewish people were "cast out" of the continuum of the dividing and divining growth process of Nature. Humans are vulnerable and not all-powerful, all-knowing, and are not vastly everywhere present. Since humans are localized in a cellular form, the Jews idealized a human-like god and projected the qualities of omniscience, omnipotence, and omnipresence to be attributes of an anthropomorphic god.

Sexuality

The origin of existence is said to be an intelligent first father, who made a first son from the soil of the earth in the image of the god. The first father from the body of his first son, made the first woman. Then occurred a further surprise! One can only ponder why the god as the first father gave the first humans genitals. If he wanted the humans to remain innocent and to only maintain the Garden of Eden, why endow them with the potential for sexuality?

Accepting that humans were made in the image of the god, as stated in Genesis 1:26-29, it can only be reasonably assumed that the god also has genitals. Since the god has genitals and created humans with genitals, (humans did not create their own genitals) there must have been some future intention for genital use.

A god who is said to have omniscience would surely not have creatively designed male and female sexual organs without some foreknowledge and intention for these parts of the human anatomy to be functionally activated and useful at some future time. Therefore, to be endowed with genitals was the obvious design and plan of the god.

The comprehension that humans were endowed with genitals made in the image of the god, also suggests a sexual meaning in the later mention of Luke 1:34-35, when Mary was told she would conceive and bear a son. "Then said Mary unto the angel, How shall this be, seeing I know not a man? And the angel answered and said unto her, The Holy Ghost shall come upon thee, and the power of the Highest shall overshadow thee." The Greek verb "episkiazo" means to "cover or overshadow," referring to clouds. The highest god who made humans in his likeness with genitals, and later covered Mary like the shadow of a cloud and came upon her, takes on much more of a sexual meaning.

While the first humans were portrayed as disobedient, they only acquired the knowledge of their human-like maker. Genesis 3:22 says, "And the Lord God said, Behold, the man is become as one of us, to know good and evil." The realization obtained from the Tree of Knowledge of Good and Evil was nudity that later led to the consequence of sexual reproduction. Genesis 3:7 states, "And the eyes of them both were opened, and they knew that they were naked; and they sewed fig leaves together, and made themselves aprons." Genesis 4:1-2 states, "And Adam knew Eve his wife; and she conceived, and bare, Cain ...And she again bare his brother Abel."

The Genesis story of human sexuality causes a problem with the primal parents Adam and Eve. The first parent situation produces a parent-child incest relationship in that generation, and also necessitates a brother-sister incest relationship in the second generation. Genesis 4:25-26, 5:1-5, states that Adam lived to be 930 years and during this time "begat sons and daughters" including Seth. Eve gave birth to Seth, but the text does not mention the mother of the other children of Adam. The scenario suggests parent-child incest, and also a brother-sister incest relationship to begin to populate the earth.

So came about an evil beginning for Hebrew humankind. In reality, sexual reproduction came into existence when the god first made life.

"And God created great whales, and every living creature that moveth, which the waters brought forth abundantly, after their kind, and every winged fowl after his kind: and God saw that it was good. And God blessed them, saying, Be fruitful, and multiply, and fill the waters in the seas, and let fowl multiply in the earth." (Genesis 1:21-22)

Since animals were sexually multiplying, they also had to consume other life forms to live. It was when the god made life that death also came into existence on the earth for plants, animals, and humans. Genesis 1:29-30 says:

"And God said, Behold, I have given you every herb bearing seed, which is upon the face of all the earth, and every tree, in the which is the fruit of a tree yielding seed; to you it shall be for meat. And to every beast of the earth, and to every fowl of the air, and to every thing that creepeth upon the earth, wherein there is life, I have given every green herb for meat: and it was so."

Eating implies that plants, animals and humans were already subject to dying for they were made with the need to consume nutrition. To sustain a living creature, the life process requires the death of another living form. Not to eat food is to surely die. A meal roughly every four or five hours is required for humans to alleviate the pangs of hunger, and if food is not obtained for an extended time, the sure death of starvation occurs. Cause is followed unerringly by effect; life eating life prolongs existence for a time, yet life must always meet with its death.

Evil

David Hume (1711-1776) in his work, *Dialogues Concerning Natural Religion*, has the following to say about questions raised by the Greek philosopher Epicurus. "Epicurus's old questions are yet unanswered. Is God willing to prevent evil, but not able? then is he impotent.

Is he able, but not willing? then is he malevolent. Is he both able and willing? whence then is evil?" A saying from the extant writings of Epicurus (341–270 BCE) regarding a god is: "A blessed and indestructible being has no trouble himself and brings no trouble upon any other being; so he is free from anger and partiality, for all such traits imply weakness." The god of the bible brings much trouble to himself and inflicts punishment on humankind. For example, Deuteronomy 6-15 states, "For the Lord thy God is a jealous God among you, lest the anger of the Lord thy God be kindled against thee, and destroy thee from off the face of the earth."

It can be assumed that a superior god who has supernatural knowledge would create only what is good, but the god of Genesis knows and creates both good and evil. Genesis 2:16-17 states that the god, after creating Adam, took the man and placed him in the Garden to keep it. He further commanded him saying that the man could eat of every tree, "But of the tree of the knowledge of good and evil, thou shalt not eat of it: for in the day that thou eatest thereof thou shalt surely die." In Genesis 3:22, the god states, "Behold, the man is become as one of us, to know good and evil: and now, lest he put forth his hand, and take also of the tree of life, and eat, and live for ever."

All things have come from the god; not only all good things but also all evil things. Since the god made humans, and they did not behave properly as he intended them, then the fault is not with the maker but how humans were made, especially the potential for genital sexuality. In Genesis 1, all of life was optimistically made to be "very good", but in a short time chapters 2-4 convey a plunge into a serious crisis, and human life soon becomes a curse of the god. The Garden of Eden tale is about blame and shame. According to the story, humans became separate from the god through acquiring knowledge of both good and evil.

The story portrays the problem with knowledge that is apparent through history and modern times, especially sexual knowledge and reproduction. One only has to look at history and the daily news to see the violence and trauma of spouse abuse, divorce, rape, and sexual exploitation.

There is also the problem of the human mind out of control, with an endless stream of knowledge as volition, memory, imagination, and emotional desires.

Genesis chapter 3 points out that the god did not freely and willingly give the knowledge of good and evil, nudity, sexuality, and reproduction to humans. But since the god placed the Tree of Knowledge of Good and Evil in the garden, this act insured that the humans had the opportunity to willfully acquire abundant knowledge. The god is portrayed as not willing to let the humans have knowledge but that it was willfully taken by humans. Since a god is all powerful and no naïve human could ever get the knowledge from him, there had to be a mechanism or some way for humans to obtain the knowledge. This was conveniently done by placing the knowledge of good and evil on a special tree. Genesis 2:9 says, "And out of the ground made the Lord God to grow every tree that is pleasant to the sight, and good for food; the tree of life also in the midst of the garden, and the tree of knowledge of good and evil."

While other pleasant looking and good tasting fruit trees were placed in the garden, the two special trees were placed among them. It would have been difficult for the naïve first humans to correctly tell which was which, and fully know the consequences thereof. The god also placed the Tree of Knowledge of Good and Evil in the center, the central emphasis of the garden. The tree of knowledge was not placed on the periphery, but in the middle, and the main focal spot of the garden. Certainly a special tree merits some special attention, especially by naïve humans. After seeing the special tree, Genesis 3:6-7 says:

"The woman saw that the tree was good for food, and that it was pleasant to the eyes, and a tree to be desired to make one wise, she took of the fruit thereof, and did eat, and gave also unto her husband with her; and he did eat. And the eyes of them both were opened, and they knew that they were naked; and they sewed fig leaves together, and made themselves aprons."

Genesis 1:29 plainly states humans were given the fruit of "every tree" to eat.

In Genesis 3, the god changes his mind and mentions there are two exceptions to the previous command. Newly created, naïve and most likely confused by conflicting commands, the first humans were also probably in conflict about fruit eating. They were assisted by a serpent in making their infamous choice that influenced later humankind. In Genesis 3 the humans were forced to leave the garden and go forth upon the earth.

Having been made "very good" in Genesis 1:31, "And God saw every thing that he had made, and, behold, it was very good", and given the freedom in Genesis 1:28 "And God blessed them, and God said unto them, Be fruitful, and multiply, and replenish the earth…" Genesis 1:26-27 says:

"And God said, Let us make man in our image, after our likeness: and let them have dominion over the fish of the sea, and over the fowl of the air, and over the cattle, and over all the earth, and over every creeping thing that creepeth upon the earth. So God created man in his own image, in the image of God created he him; male and female created he them."

Being made in the image of the god, blessed and told to be fruitful and multiply, humans must have had, at that time, the knowledge to carry out the command of the god. At the end of Genesis 1, the god gave the command to "be fruitful and multiply," and so confirms that the first humans were endowed from the beginning with the knowledge of nudity, sexuality, and reproduction. Yet in Genesis chapters 2-4, humans are portrayed as being without the knowledge of how to be fruitful and to multiply, in contrast to the first chapter. In Genesis chapters 2-4, the god made humans with a basic naiveté, and there was a complete lack of any kind of exceptional knowledge including evil. There was nil capacity to recognize the presence of evil, so the first humans had to assume that even the serpent was good. Innocent humans did not have a clue as to the evil ability of the serpent to deceive. Having been made "very good," trusting humans expected only good.

While the god warned the humans about the evil-containing fruit from the Tree of Knowledge of Good and Evil, he did not warn them of the evil and tempting serpent.

The god created the evil within the serpent that easily convinced the humans to taste an appealing fruit containing evil. What was the gods' intention for the Tree of Knowledge of Good and Evil? The god directly transmitted the evil knowledge within himself into the tree, and also into the serpent. With the god arranging all conditions, the appealing tree fruit and the persuading serpent, humans did not have a prayer of a chance. Genesis 3:1 says, "Now the serpent was more subtil than any beast of the field which the Lord God had made." So the serpent scenario begs the question of who is more to blame; the evil knowing god who made the evil tempting serpent, or naïve and innocent humans who had limited and inferior knowledge.

But why a special tree and fruit? In language, a root is a synonym for a cause, such as the phrase a "root cause." A fruit is the end result of growth, and a synonym for an effect. The tree represents the growth and development from cause to effect. All things as fruits of existence are traced back to a cause; in this case the god. The god is the ultimate cause of making available the effect of evil. To live, humans also needed the fruit, had to consume other life forms and reproduce. Metaphorically, the evil act of tasting the fruit represents the consuming of the offspring of living plants and animals as food. It is also a metaphor for being fruitful and multiplying, and of reproduction, or "fruit of the womb" that brings the necessity of death. Both acts of eating and reproducing bring the heart-rending experience of death to the earth. The serpent is the disowned and disguised symbol of the god's male penis, and in reality the human penis, which persuades the female first into the awareness of her nudity followed by sexual reproduction.

In contrast to the Tree of Knowledge of Good and Evil, the Tree of Life had a fruit that endowed immortality. Why make this special tree? What did the god intend for it? That humans could exist forever like the god? Humans did not obtain this knowledge, as the god successfully deprived them of the knowledge of living forever. This had to be so, as to "live and be forever" are mutually exclusive concepts. A life existence as a relative time process of motion and change excludes a state of forever.

Genesis 3:22 says, "And the Lord God said, Behold, the man is become as one of us, to know good and evil: and now, lest he put forth his hand, and take also of the tree of life, and eat, and live for ever." But to be living and have knowledge of the good and evil of eating other life forms, nudity, sexual reproduction and death are necessary and innate correlations of the life process.

The god refused to let humans have abundant knowledge but he did allow them to see and have access to a tree from which they could acquire it through the ingestion of a fruit. However, the god brought the serpent into existence; the serpent did not create itself. It was through the god that the serpent came to exist, so the willing of the god is implicated. Via this mechanism, it was the will of the god for humans to have the knowledge of good and evil, of nudity, sexuality and reproduction, and death. The serpent was only the stooge (one who plays a subordinate and compliant role to one in charge) of the god.

In Genesis 2, there is the first mention of the presence of evil placed by the god on the special Tree of Knowledge of Good and Evil. There was not a special tree of good knowledge or a special tree of evil knowledge. This means that good and evil are necessarily related. The second mention of evil is the subtle serpent. The god made the serpent that tempted the first naïve and good humans who had little basic knowledge, into having the fruit. The third mention of evil is that which was inflicted as punishment by the god who began a sequence of curses. As defined in the dictionary, a curse (Hebrew, arar) as a noun is a "prayer or invocation for harm or injury to come upon one, evil or misfortune that comes as retribution." As a verb, to curse means, "to call upon divine or supernatural power to send injury upon, to bring great evil upon." So the god proceeded to curse, and bring evil first upon the serpent, the woman second, and lastly the man.

Theologians like to emphasize that humans were endowed by a human-like god with a "free will." The cause of human disobedience cannot be based on a free will. The first humans had no free will, as they had little knowledge and they were in a controlled environment.

Since the god clearly knows good and evil, and placed it where humans with minimal knowledge could easily access it, then one has to question who has the greater responsibility; the parent god or the innocent human children? It was the god who formed the evil serpent of the field from the earth, just as the god formed Adam from the earth and formed Eve from the man. Since the first humans were made in the god's image, the evil was innate within them.

The Genesis story records that Adam and Eve were innocent and naïve in the Garden, and even after being cursed and banished to labor on the earth, they did not display aggression. Yet their son Cain did have the knowledge of how to kill his brother Abel. The evil knowledge of taking a life is also plainly a god-like knowledge and behavior. Just after the listing of the generations in Genesis 5, there is the prelude to a great evil act; that of the parent-god cursing and killing his human children with the flood. Genesis 6:5-7 states:

"And God saw that the wickedness of man was great in the earth, and that every imagination of the thoughts of his heart was only evil continually. And it repented the Lord that he had made man on the earth, and it grieved him at his heart. And the Lord said, I will destroy man whom I have created from the face of the earth; both man, and beast, and the creeping thing, and the fowls of the air; for it repenteth me that I have made them."

These are the words of the punishing god, Yhwh. The Hebrew word for sin (Old Norse and English synn) is "hata,' or separation from the origin of existence through a hurtful fault. The English word repent (Hebrew nacham) means to "turn aside from sin." The first mention of an individual repenting in the bible is the god Yhwh, who repents in Genesis 6:6, and also later in Exodus 32:14. The god is the first biblical personality to repent. Adam, Eve or Cain did not repent, nor did any other human in Genesis.

While the god repents his making of life, he does not accept responsibility for the presence of good and evil knowledge within him, nor the making of the Tree of Knowledge of Good and Evil, or the subtle evil serpent that he had formed.

The god did repent for making humans, as they were out of control caused by the capacity for both good and evil acquired through the ingestion of the fruit of knowledge that he had made. Humans chose less good and much more evil as the god observed in Genesis 6:11-12 that the "imagination of the thoughts of his heart was only evil continually."

God repented for making humans and all of animal life as well, since "all flesh" was corrupted by "violence" upon the earth. No explanation is given as to how animal life became violent and therefore corrupt. The continual evil of humans cannot be exclusive to willful disobedience, but to the agent. Therefore the god admirably and deservedly repents, and then, (since the god's love plays no part in this scenario) uses his ability for evil force to destroy life.

In the Garden story, humans are portrayed as innocent and as coming into existence as completely good. Then, through the choice of willing disobedience, they entered into the existential reality of struggle and suffering. But looking closer, it is easy to see that humans were not made completely innocent, as the parent god was not innocent and completely good. A pre-existing tendency, an innate trait for evil, was inherited and passed down from the parent to the child. To be made in the image of the god, and commanded to go out and be fruitful and multiply and have dominion over the earth in Chapter 1, implies that humans were endowed from the beginning with a god-like will to accomplish the ordered tasks.

Genesis 2:19-20 states that the man was given an intelligent capacity only of naming animals; "And out of the ground the Lord God formed every beast of the field, and every fowl of the air; and brought them unto Adam to see what he would call them: and whatsoever Adam called every living creature, that was the name thereof. And Adam gave names to all cattle, and to the fowl of the air, and to every beast of the field."

Free Will

Modern theologians insist that humans were, and are, endowed with a free will. A will is never free, it is always influenced by conditions, as evidenced by the Garden of Eden narrative. The first man had no free will of his own as Genesis 2:15 states, "And the Lord God took the man, and put him into the garden of Eden to dress it and to keep it." The man was placed in a special garden only to keep up the place, and had no knowledge of good or any instruction except what was provided by the god.

The serpent was made and endowed by the god with subtle knowledge and the ability to lie and influence humans. Genesis 3:4-5 says, "And the serpent said unto the woman, Ye shall not surely die: For God doth know that in the day ye eat thereof, then your eyes shall be opened, and ye shall be as gods, knowing good and evil." The god had primary knowledge of good and evil, and the serpent secondary knowledge. Humans were made innocent without evil knowledge, and therefore only made an innocent choice to eat the fruit. Only after acquiring god-like knowledge were they no longer innocent and had a will capable of good and evil choices.

In the Genesis story there was no loving correction by the god of his innocent and naïve offspring who ate the fruit. In the entire book of Genesis, there is no mention of love by the god for humans. Just as some earthly fathers are punitive, neglectful, unloving, and can abandon their offspring, the Hebrew god did so from the beginning.

If humans have a fault, as stated in Genesis 3:6, it is in wanting something "pleasant to the eyes…good for food" to eat, and to gain some god-like knowledge. With humans, it is innate to always enjoy a good meal, to be curious and like to learn. In the Genesis story, evil came from the god who knows what evil is, he created it, and placed it along with good on a special earthly tree. When the god cast out the humans from the Garden, he said, "Behold, the man is become as one of us, to know good and evil…." (Gen 3:22) This statement convincingly shows that the ability the evil humans have within them is a god-like and inherited from their maker.

Evil

Edward Conklin

What is evil? I define evil as an "excessive force, that disrupts and harms." This can first be observed in the function of the environment, in such disruptive events as earthquakes, floods, asteroid and comet impact, and extremes of drought or cold weather. At the basic level of life, viruses and bacteria exist, most of which are not harmful but in sufficient numbers can and do cause serious diseases. There are multi-cellular organisms like fish, insects, reptiles and mammals that continually use aggressive force to consume other plant and animal species while the prey is still alive.

Genesis1:12, 21, 30 states that the god made the grasses, trees, whales, fish, fowl, and every beast of the earth and humans, and told them to multiply. How did every living creature survive to be fruitful and multiply, without the evil excessive force of aggression? Life cannot reproduce without food, so the evil of aggression is an inherent affirmation of life. Humans are a continuum of environmental, plant, and animal behaviors, and utilize both physical and mental excessive force of aggression much more than any other species. These forceful behaviors include lies and insults, exploitation, assault, crime, homicide, war, and genocide. Excessive force is present in all kinds of fatal and nonfatal accidents. This is life, and nothing will ever change it; not any god of any culture on the earth, but only the evolution of wisdom, or the eventual extinction of the species.

What was the intention for creating evil and placing it where humans could have a chance to access it? Was the tree just a place to store evil on earth in order to utilize it at some future time? Was the tree an obedience test by an all-knowing god for dependent, newly created, and wholly ignorant humans? The god, serpent, human interactive situation to explain why humans have knowledge of reproduction, and the knowledge of killing and consuming other life forms, is poorly contrived. It is difficult to accept that so many human minds, from theologians to the mass of common people, have accepted this simplistic allegorical story as true.

In Genesis, the god did not give the fruit of good and evil knowledge to humans. The god only provided the tree.

The humans took the fruit for themselves from a tree that the innocent and blameless god placed in the Garden. Humans are responsible for having this knowledge, not the god. Yet it was the god who made the Tree of Knowledge of Good and Evil so easy to access. Humans did not know of evil, did not create evil, nor did they bring evil to the earth.

Humans were created in the image or the likeness of the god. Therefore, being made in the image of the god, the ability for evil was innate. The god formed humans in his own image, and so in reality it was only a matter of time before they began to choose good and evil. Humans had no free will in creating their own existence and character. Thus human separation or sin was predestined by an omnipotent evil-capable god.

Isaiah 45:5-7 states:
"I am the Lord, and there is none else, there is no god beside me: I girded thee, though thou hast not known me: That they may know from the rising of the sun, and from the west, that there is none beside me. I am the Lord, and there is none else. I form the light, and create darkness: I make peace, and create evil: I the Lord do all these things."

Here one must applaud the truth and honesty of the literary born god. In later Christian theology, the god created angels in his image. One of them, the angel Satan, utilized his innate ability for evil to oppose the god and convince other angels to rebel. So the evil force of aggression is innate and present even in godly angels.

Social Order

The traditional attempt to keep order in a social group is either by the rule of a leader that evolved into government, or by rule of a leader that evolved into religion. Written laws, like religious writings, serve to instill social order. No human-like god has ever spoken and acted to bring about social order. Historically, only a prophet has spoken and recorded the words of a deity.

Religious scholars, beginning in 1700 CE, have recognized many contradictions and differing traditions of biblical writings.

Israelites from northern Israel (circa 800 BCE), began writing versions of social events and eventually were added to form the Bible. The writings, in which the god is called El and Elohim, make up about one-third of Genesis and about one-half of Exodus, and a portion of the book of Numbers. The Elohim writings focus more on the history and events in northern Israel and the priesthood established there.

Rabbis from the southern area of Judah began to write sections of the bible (circa 700 BCE) that resemble those writings of the earlier El or Elohim authors, but here the god is called Yhwh. The Yhwh writings make about up half of Genesis and probably about half of Exodus, and includes some portions of the book of Numbers. There is a special focus on the history of the land in Judah, and individuals associated with events there.

The book of Deuteronomy was written (circa 600 BCE) in Jerusalem, and refers to god as Yhwh-Elohainu, which is translated into English as "the Lord our God." Deuteronomy means "second law," and the book contains three speeches said to have been made by Moses. The first speech tells of wandering in the wilderness, the second comments on obligations, and the third speaks on what the god will do for Judah. It includes a retelling of the commandments, mentions many other commandments, and the death of Moses.

The "shema" is found in the book of Deuteronomy 6:4, and is the important statement of creed in Judaism. In Hebrew, the verse is "Shema Yisrael Adonai Eloheinu Adonai Ehad," which translates to English as "Hear, O Israel: The Lord our God is one Lord." The word shema means to hear or to listen, while yisrael are "the people of Israel." Adonai means "lord." Eloheinu means, "our god," and "ehad" means a numerical one, or the word "only." Other translations are; "Hear, O Israel! Adonai is our God! Adonai is One" and "Hear, O Israel! Adonai is our God, Adonai alone." The verse is distinctly emphatic that the worshipped god El is the only and exclusive god of the Israelites and no other human group.

The priestly writings date from 550-400 BCE during, or shortly after the Babylonian Exile, and show a concern with the priesthood, laws, genealogies, dates, and numbers.

The priestly writers contributed about a fourth of the book of Genesis, parts of the books of Exodus and Numbers, and nearly the entire book of Leviticus. There are a total of 613 commandments given by the two god traditions scattered through a number of bible books. What are known as the Ten Commandments are mentioned in three differing versions; in the book of Exodus 20:2-17, Exodus 34:11-27, and the book of Deuteronomy 5:6-21.

Circa 700 BCE, there was a first redaction, editing, combining, and minor changing of the Old Testament books. A second redaction occurred circa 600 BCE, and a third took place circa 400 BCE that arranged the work in its present format. The writings of the Tanak, or Old Testament, are intended to explain the origin of the environment and life, good and evil, and human struggle and suffering. The writings also present the commandments given by the god and various prophets to serve as a social guide to reduce struggle, conflict and suffering in the lives of the Jews. To date there has obviously been little success in this regard.

Brief History

During the 1300's BCE, there were bedouin clan groups known variously as the Ibri, Apiru, and Shosu living in the highland region of southern Canaan. They posed a threat to the Canaanite ruler of the time, as they raided the sparse, settled communities of southern Canaan. When these clan groups are mentioned in the Akkadian cuneiform Tell el-Amarna letters dated to 1300's BCE, they are said to be lawless mercenaries, and working as paid laborers in Egypt. One or both of these groups were probably the indigenous ancestors of the people later known as "the Hebrews and Israelites." The earliest brief mention of a distinct group of people known as Israelites living in Canaan is found on the Egyptian Merneptah victory stele, dated circa 1207 BCE.

While both Judah and Israel share a common patriarchal origin, the archaeological artifacts support the view that the two groups were never united under one rule. There is much linguistic evidence that the god of northern Israel was El and the southern tribe of Judah worshiped the god Yhwh.

After the defeat of northern Israel by the Assyrians in 722 BCE, the god El was eventually displaced and subsumed by Yhwh, the god of southern Judah. This is evident in Exodus 6:2-3, which is a priestly insertion or redaction dating to the late 500's and early 400's BCE. "And God said to Moses, I am Yahweh. I appeared to Abraham, to Isaac, and to Jacob, as El Shadday, but by my name Yahweh I did not make myself known to them."

The combined El and Yhwh traditions are responsible for the glaring verse contradictions, such as seeing the god: "And the Lord said unto Moses, Go down, charge the people, lest they break through unto the Lord to gaze, and many of them perish...And Moses said unto the Lord, The people cannot come up to mount Sinai: for thou chargedst us, saying, Set bounds about the mount, and sanctify it." (Exodus 19: 21, 23) In another version some of the people did see the god and did not perish. "Then went up Moses, and Aaron, Nadab, and Aibihu, and seventy of the elders of Israel: And they saw the God of Israel: and there was under his feet as it were a paved work of a sapphire stone, and as it were the body of heaven in his clearness. And upon the nobles of the children of Israel he laid not his hand: also they saw God, and did eat and drink." (Exodus 24:9-11)

The Book of Numbers states that the god of the Exodus was El rather than Yhwh. "God brought them out of Egypt; he hath as it were the strength of an unicorn." (Numbers 23:22) A later more accurate scholarly translation of these verses is, "El who freed them from Egypt has horns like a wild ox.

The northern ruler Jeroboam II (788 - 747 BCE) states that it was the god El who led the Israelites out of Egypt.

"Whereupon the king took counsel, and made two calves of gold, and said unto them, it is too much for you to go up to Jerusalem: behold thy gods, O'Isrsel, which brought thee up out of the land of Egypt. And he set the one in Bethel, and the other put he in Dan...And Jeroboam ordained a feast in the eighth month, on the fifteenth day of the month, like unto the feast that is in Judah, and he offered upon the altar. So did he in Bethel, sacrificing unto the calves that he had made: and he placed in Bethel the priests of the high places which he had made." (Kings 12:28-29, 32)

Of course, the Judahite writer of 1 Kings 12:30 whose god is Yhwh sees golden calf worship as a sin. "And this thing became a sin: for the people went to worship before the one, even unto Dan."

The book of 2 Kings Chapter 23 makes it plain that the transition from polytheism to the monotheism of Yhwh was politically imposed in 622 BCE by the Judahite ruler Josaih.

In 622 BCE, as renovations were being made to the temple in Jerusalem, the "book of the law" was discovered. (2 Kings 22:8-23:24) This event began a severe religious reform by the Judahite ruler Josiah, and marked the politically imposed transition from polytheism to monotheism. Scholars think the found document was the book of Deuteronomy, which does show evidence of being written during this time. After finding the scroll, a temple priest read it to Josiah (2 Kings 22:8-10) who ordered and did the following:

"And the king commanded Hilkiah the high priest, and the priests of the second order, and the keepers of the door, to bring forth out of the temple of the Lord all the vessels that were made for Baal, and for the grove, and for all the host of heaven: and he burned them without Jerusalem in the fields of Kidron, and carried the ashes of them unto Bethel. And he put down the idolatrous priests, whom the kings of Judah had ordained to burn incense in the high places in the cities of Judah, and in the places round about Jerusalem; them also that burned incense unto Baal, to the sun, and to the moon, and to the planets, and to all the host of heaven…And he brake down the houses of the sodomites that were by the house of the Lord, where the women wove hangings for the grove...." (2 Kings 23:4-5, 7)

"And he defiled Topheth, which is in the valley of the children of Hinnom, that no man might make his son or his daughter to pass through the fire to Molech. And he took away the horses that the kings of Judah had given to the sun, at the entering in of the house of the Lord, by the chamber of Nathanmelech the chamberlain, which was in the suburbs, and burned the chariots of the sun with fire…And the high places that were before Jerusalem, which were on the right hand of the mount of corruption.

Which Solomon the king of Israel had built for Ashtoreth the abomination of the Zidonians, and for Chemosh the abomination of the Moabites, and for Milcom the abomination of the children of Ammon, did the king defile. And he brake in pieces the images, and cut down the groves, and filled their places with the bones of men...." (2 Kings 23:10-11, 13-14) "Moreover the workers with familiar spirits, and the wizards, and the images, and the idols, and all the abominations that were spied in the land of Judah and in Jerusalem, did Josiah put away...." (2 Kings 23:24)

The worship of these many mentioned gods had been sanctioned by early Judahite as well as Israelite rulers. Baal was the Phoenician sun god who was widely worshiped in both Judah and Israel. Solomon built an altar near Jerusalem for the worship of the god of the Moabites, named Chemosh and to whom the Jews sacrificed their children as burnt offerings in fire. (1 Kings 11:7) Milcom was another name for the Ammonite god Molech who was worshiped at an altar at the high place of Topheth in the valley of Hinnom. The Judahite rulers Ahaz (743-727 BCE) and Manasseh (698-642 BCE) worshiped this god and sacrificed their children there as burnt offerings (2 Chronicles 28:3; 2 Kings 21:6). The peoples of both Judah and Israel sacrificed their children from circa 900 BCE until the reform of Josaih 622 BCE.

Verse 7 says, "And he brake down the houses of the sodomites...." The male prostitutes of the temple offered communion with one or more of the gods through sexual intercourse. The women wove hangings for the grove worship of the goddess of fertility, Asherah or Ashtoreth of Sidon. In the temple was an upright piece of wood that represented her that was placed beside the altar of the god Baal. Jeroboam II, ruler of Israel (788-747 BCE), had ordered the worship of two golden calves or bulls at Bethel and Dan. (1 Kings 12: 28-31)

Objects of worship of Baal, Asherah, and the "host of heaven" were placed in the temple of Yhwh in Jerusalem. Ezekiel 8:14-16 mentions the god Tammuz was worshiped by women at the "door of the gate of the Lord's house," and male worshipers at the door of the temple faced east while worshiping the sun.

Mentioned in 2 Kings 23:24, the "workers with familiar spirits" were mediums who claimed to be able to communicate with the deceased. A "wizard" was someone who delivered oracles. The mentioned idols were of various deities, some were known as "teraphim" and were associated with worship of the moon.

Soul and Resurrection

The Hebrew word "ruah" means variously, breath, blowing, or moving air. Genesis 1:2 says, "And the earth was without form, and void; and darkness was upon the face of the deep. And the Spirit [ruah] of God moved upon the face of the waters." Genesis 7:15 says "And they went in unto Noah into the ark, two and two of all flesh, wherein is the breath [ruah] of life." In the former reference, the god breathed or moved the air over the water, while the latter refers to the animals that were breathing and living on the ark.

Genesis 2:7 states, "And the Lord God formed man of the dust of the ground, and breathed into his nostrils the breath of life; and man became a living soul." The phrase translated here as, living soul, is the Hebrew word "nephesh," more akin in meaning to the Latin word anima, meaning, animated and alive. The first use of the word is in Genesis 1:21, which says, "And God created great whales, and every living creature [nephesh] that moveth, which the waters brought forth abundantly, after their kind, and every winged fowl after his kind: and God saw that it was good." According to this usage, animals were animated and alive, as are humans. The second use of the word is in Genesis 1:24; "And God said, Let the earth bring forth the living creature [nephesh] after his kind, cattle, and creeping thing, and beast of the earth after his kind: and it was so."

In Genesis 2:19, animals are also referred to as being nephesh. "Whatsoever Adam called every living creature [nephesh] that was the name thereof." In Genesis 9:4, 5 it states that what animates life is not a soul but the blood. "But flesh with the life [nephesh] thereof, which is the blood thereof, shall ye not eat. And surely your blood of your lives [nephesh] will I require; at the hand of every beast will I require it, and at the hand of man; at the hand of every man's brother will I require the life [nephesh] of man."

Both humans and animals have a life consisting of the breath and the blood, and after physical death all go to the same place, the soil of the earth. Modern theists tend to think of themselves as better than animals. Christians especially think that humans go to a special place after physical death that excludes animals.

"For that which befalleth the sons of men befalleth beasts; even one thing befalleth them: as the one dieth, so dieth the other; yea, they have all one breath [ruah] so that a man hath no preeminence above a beast: for all is vanity. All go unto one place; all are of the dust, and all to dust return again." (Ecclesiastes 3:19-20)

In every culture there are ways of dealing with the inevitable experience of death. In Jewish thought, the earliest conception of what happened to humans after physical death was "sheol,' meaning, a pit located beneath the earth. The Jews had no concept of a soul or spirit that could go on to other afterlife dimensions including heaven hell, or reincarnation. The main reality was the physical body, and when dead, the nonphysical shadow of the person would journey to Sheol. Of Sheol it is said, "For the living know that they shall die: but the dead know not any thing, neither have they any more a reward; for the memory of them is forgotten." (Ecclesiastes 9: 5) In early days, death was referred to as sleep, and this is mentioned in the Tanak. "And the Lord said unto Moses, Behold, thou shalt sleep with thy fathers." (Deuteronomy 31:16) "Otherwise it shall come to pass, when my lord the king shall sleep with his fathers, that I and my son Solomon shall be counted offenders." (1 Kings 1:21) "So man lieth down, and riseth not: till the heavens [be] no more, they shall not awake, nor be raised out of their sleep." (Job 14:12)

In 586 BCE, the Babylonians conquered Judea, and deported most of the population to Babylon. The man who came to be known as Cyrus the Great, was born circa 580 BCE in Persia, now Iran. Circa 558 BCE he succeeded his father to become ruler of the Persian Empire. In 539 BCE the Babylonian Empire, including Syria and Palestine, surrendered to Cyrus without going to battle. In 537 BCE, Cyrus allowed the Jews to return to Judea, and sent workers to help them rebuild the temple in Jerusalem. For this gesture the Jews called him "messiah," meaning, anointed one.

The view of resurrection was brought to the Jews during this time by a follower of Zoroastrian religion, the ruler Cyrus the Great.

"Thus saith the Lord to his anointed, to Cyrus, whose right hand I have holden, to subdue nations before him; and I will loose the loins of kings, to open before him the two leaved gates; and the gates shall not be shut; I will go before thee, and make the crooked places straight: I will break in pieces the gates of brass, and cut in sunder the bars of iron: And I will give thee the treasures of darkness, and hidden riches of secret places, that thou mayest know that I, the Lord, which call thee by thy name, am the God of Israel." (Isaiah 45:1-3)

The earliest biblical mention of resurrection is found in the book of Isaiah, and dates to circa 334 BCE:

"Thy dead men shall live, together with my dead body shall they arise. Awake and sing, ye that dwell in dust: for thy dew is as the dew of herbs, and the earth shall cast out the dead…For, behold, the Lord cometh out of his place to punish the inhabitants of the earth for their iniquity: the earth also shall disclose her blood, and shall no more cover her slain." (26:19, 21)

Like the primitive conception of Sheol, and death as sleep, the resurrection is also a crude Mideast fable of the coming back to life again, and arising of the once-only physical body.

Comments

It's all about time. The Bible books are a poetic attempt to express stories portrayed as history. Historical memories of experience then become optimism or pessimism, and a bifurcation into a dual struggle of good and evil. Judaism lacked a technique for exploration of now time, and opted for a quasi-historical time composed of a series of misinterpreted and imagined events. History became tradition, which in turn became the later legalism of the 613 ritual commandments, in a superficial social attempt to improve the quality of life experience. No technique was ever developed to increase observation of the present, such as yoga and meditation practices.

Jesus of Nazareth was a northern Israelite who was likely influenced by Eastern thinking and disciplines. He taught the practice of love, which centered the individual in now moments of time, pragmatically useful in reducing the distracting and traumatic effects of life. Looking forward to the future of an afterlife in a heaven further removes an individual from historical thinking. Being an Israelite, it was inevitable that Jesus would continue to use the projection of a human-like father god. While comforting to listeners, this unfortunate way of thinking contributed to directing attention outward and away from observation and exploration of mental and physical functions occurring in now moments of time. The god met the deceased in a future afterlife was also interested in the historical identity of the individual, which was important and valued as it was used to determine reward and punishment.

It is always shocking when an educated person like James Irwin (1930-1991), a former American astronaut and one of eight persons to set foot on the moon, accept what is plainly religious myth as reality and fact. From 1973-1982, Irwin led several expeditions to Turkey to search for the remains of Noah's Ark. Of course, he and all others have failed in the search for an ark for a simple realistic reason. There never was one.

## Chapter 6

*And the day will come when the mystical generation of Jesus, by the supreme being as his father in the womb of a virgin will be classed with the fable of the generation of Minerva in the brain of Jupiter.*
*Thomas Jefferson*

## Christianity

Jesus attempted in his own culture to solve the problem of human existence. Jesus, like Moses before him, and theistic successor Muhammad, saw the political and social order as evil, the religious order as oppressive, and each thought only a human-like god could change earthly conditions. Humans had to relate to someone or something, higher and greater than themselves to bring about beneficial individual and social change.

Tracing existence back to a first cause, sans math and science, early knowledge-limited humans could only identify it as human-like. Early humans of the Middle East lacked the capacity to perceive the origin of existence to be a nonhuman cosmic force generating energy elements into inanimate and animate forms. Seeking an unknown first cause, must through necessity reach a terminus of something unknown that must be known. For most early human cultures the first cause must be known as human-like. The first cause had to be a greater knowledgeable maker of the environment, and though not human, had to resemble humans. Human experience of wonder and the cognitive demand to identify an incomprehensible first cause of existence, it was made comprehensible to humans by conceiving a first parent of humankind.

The Christian view of the origin of existence is based on family structure; a god as father, Mary is the human mother, and Jesus is the god's questionable human son. Christianity promotes the parent-child relationship more so than any other religion, and so it appeals primarily to women and to families.

The religion teaches the importance of the practice of love and forgiveness among family members, and the larger human family of the community and country. Jesus promoted love of the shared origin as a greater father figure god, and also promoted shared human love; "Thou shalt love the Lord thy God with all thy heart, and with all thy soul, and with all thy mind. This is the first and greatest commandment. And the second is like unto it; Thou shalt love thy neighbour as thyself."(Matthew 22:37-39)

What could be better than to be a member of a religion that promises the individual that in spite of the traumatic experience of life and mistreatment by fellow humans, each would continue to have the support and love of a heavenly father? Additionally, what could be better than the promise that after death, one would be a member of a greater family community of the elect, with the eternal protection of a father-like god in the afterlife of a heaven? Christianity is based on the family structure of the very first father as a human-like god, the son Jesus, and his mother Mary. If one joins the religion, they too will be part of the special family and not of the wicked earth, and a family of many evil people. This is the religion's main appeal. By joining the Christian religion, the person will be a member of an afterlife good family, and no longer a member of the excessively evil earthly family. The first father human-like god will be there in the afterlife, along with his son Jesus and his saintly mother Mary.

Christianity has the most adherents of any religion, nearly one third of the earth's population. The success of Christianity has to be correctly attributed to cognitive immaturity of adults, in which the origin of existence is metaphorically identified as a human-like father and hypostasized as real.

Christianity is based on an individual's relationship with a human father, and the need for approval and love. Sigmund Freud also attributed the origin of Christianity to the Oedipus complex of childhood. The child's emotional need to please an earthly father is continued into adulthood, in order to please the theistic personality of a greater father-like god.

During the time of Jesus, the Jews were in relationship with the harsh paternal Jewish and Roman governments.

Since these parental governments demonstrated little love for the people, attention was directed to a supernatural parent located in a heaven. The forefather god would care for them in life and eventually welcome them after death when they would finally be comforted and loved. Yet what heavenly father, while interested in the events of the earth, could bear to watch the agony of his earthly children being torn apart by wild animals in Roman arenas?

Since the earthly governing fathers were strict, dominating, and cruel, Jesus taught; "And call no man your father upon the earth: for one is your Father, which is in heaven." (Matthew 23:9) His statement is a rejection of the abusive, conflict-ridden values of earthly fathers. Instead, love is sought in the acceptance of an idealized conception of a first father god. Accepting the idea of a human-like father god provides parental love, guidance, and a future order. A heavenly father provides partial relief from troubles and sorrows of earthly life, and serves to turn the individual away from struggles. The individual turns toward an acceptance of one's own eventual death and transition to where the good family of humankind will continue to exist without struggle in an afterlife. The challenge for faith (Latin fidere, trust) is to sustain this conceived view or belief. Since the earthly father continues to be even more irresponsible and cruel through modern times, and the heavenly father does not act upon the earth, humankind continues to struggle and to suffer, and will do so in the future.

Theo-morphism

Seeing Jesus as the son of a god is a final step or ultimate stage in the cognitive process of anthropomorphism. There is a completion of the projection; a return from a human-like god distant from humans back to a god-like human being on earth. The origin of existence was projected to be a human-like god out there, and then the reverse process of theo-morphism was imposed on a human on earth.

A god with a half human son also further confirms the existence of the god and is a way of bringing a faraway deity closer to humans. Rather than make offerings or pray to a distant deity, the offspring of a god actually existing on the earth at some historical time with eyewitnesses and story, is more real to Christians.

Earlier gods and goddesses of various religions gave birth to other deities, so why not give birth to half human offspring. Part human offspring of a human parent and a god parent are very common in other religions and mythologies. In the Mesopotamian Epic of Gilgamesh, dating from circa 2500 BCE, the father of Gilgamesh was a human priest and his mother was Ninsun, a goddess who was skilled at interpreting dreams. For the Greeks, the father of the hero Hercules was said to be Zeus, and his mother was a human by the name of Alcmene.

Atonement

While the birth of Jesus as the son of a human-like god provided a more intimate connection with the distant deity, the death of Jesus also provided a connection with the god as father through atonement. The popular scholar of religion, Huston Smith, once commented that the Christian doctrine of atonement is an "unpalatable subject." This is so, as the teaching of atonement cannot be considered a rational view. God's plan was to have a son and eventually have him be killed by humans. Only by killing his son, could the god prevent himself from judging humans after their physical death for the separation in the Garden of Eden. By killing his son he would thereby save humans from the eternal punishment and torture he would inflict upon them in the afterlife. This is very irrational thinking.

According to Christian theology, God's plan was to send his offspring, Jesus, to die as an atonement, meaning "to reconcile, or to make at one" for the sins of humankind. In Catholic services, Jesus and his death is referred to as, "The lamb of God who takes away the sins of the world." (John 1:29)

The death of Jesus was interpreted as being able to take away the sins of the world. This is shown in words attributed to Paul in I Colossians 1:19-20. "For it pleased the Father that in him should all fulness dwell; and having made peace through the blood of his cross by him to reconcile all things unto himself, by him, I say, whether they be things in earth, or things in heaven."

If the Jews could not be reconciled and at peace with their neighbor, other groups of Jews, members of the Jewish religion and government, or the Roman occupation, then they could at least be reconciled and at peace with the human-like god. In death they would have no fear.

I Corinthians 5:7-8 says, "For Christ, our paschal lamb, has been sacrificed. Let us therefore celebrate the festival, not with the old leaven, the leaven of malice and evil, but with the unleavened bread of sincerity and truth." II Corinthians 5:19 states, "God was in Christ reconciling the world to Himself, not counting their trespasses against them and entrusting to us the message of reconciliation." The word paschal comes from a Hebrew word meaning "passing over." In Exodus 12: 3-11, the god Yhwh gave instructions to Moses to protect the Hebrews from the last of the ten inflictions upon the Egyptians; the death of the firstborn.

On the tenth day of the first month, each family (or group of families) was commanded to take a lamb without blemish, male, one year old, and keep it until the fourteenth day of the month, then slaughter it in the evening. The blood of the lamb was sprinkled on the transom and doorposts of the houses in which the paschal meal is taken. The lamb was to be roasted and eaten with unleavened bread or matzo and wild lettuce.

"For I will pass through the land of Egypt this night, and will smite all the firstborn in the land of Egypt, both man and beast; and against all the gods of Egypt I will execute judgment: I am the Lord. And the blood shall be to you for a token upon the houses where ye are: and when I see the blood, I will pass over you, and the plague shall not be upon you to destroy you, when I smite the land of Egypt. And this day shall be unto you for a memorial; and ye shall keep it a feast to the Lord throughout your generations; ye shall keep it a feast by an ordinance for ever." (Exodus 12:12-14)

Other verses also confirm the Christian view that the death of the godly son Jesus was meant to take away the sins of the world. "But God shows His love for us in that while we were yet sinners, Christ died for us.

Since, therefore, we are now justified by His blood, much more shall we be saved by Him from the wrath of God." (Romans 5:8-9)

"Then as one man's trespass led to condemnation for all men so one man's act of righteousness leads to acquittal and life for all men. For as by man's disobedience [Adam] many were made sinners, so by one man's obedience [Jesus] many will be made righteous." (Romans 5:18, 19)

"For God has done what the law, weakened by flesh, could not do: sending His own Son in the likeness of sinful flesh, and for sin, He condemned sin in the flesh, in order that the just requirement of the law might be fulfilled in us, who walk not according to the flesh but according to the Spirit." (Romans 8:3, 4)

"For Christ died for sins once for all, the righteous for the unrighteous, that He might bring us to God." (I Peter 3:18) "In this is love, not that we loved God, but that He loved us and sent His Son to be the expiation for our sins." (I John 4:19)

Why would an all-powerful god want offspring in human form? The Christian answer is so the god could arrange to have humans kill his son, and the god could receive his son's blood. In this way there was an atonement, or a joining of the life that is in the blood (Leviticus 17:14) with the origin of life. In this Christian view, one is through the death of the son vicariously joined with the god as father. Since Jesus was born of a woman, through the sacrifice of his human life blood, a reconnecting link of atonement or "at one-ment" of humans occurs with the god. In this way humans are no longer in danger of the sin of separation and punishment. This Christian doctrine of atonement is based on the older Jewish ritual Day of Atonement known as Yom Kippur, as directed by the god in the book of Leviticus.

"Then Aaron shall cast lots for the two goats: one lot for the Lord and the other lot for the scapegoat. And Aaron shall bring the goat on which the Lord's lot fell, and offer it as a sin offering.

But the goat on which the lot fell to be the scapegoat shall be presented alive before the Lord, to make atonement upon it, and to let it go as the scapegoat into the wilderness...Aaron shall lay both his hands on the head of the live goat, confess over it all the iniquities of the children of Israel, and all their transgressions, concerning all their sins, putting them on the head of the goat, and shall send it away into the wilderness by the hand of a suitable man. The goat shall bear on itself all their iniquities to an uninhabited land; and he shall release the goat in the wilderness." (16:8-10, 21-22)

After the confessing of, and transferring of sins, via the laying of hands on the scapegoat, the animal was taken out and thrown over a cliff and killed. If the goat lived and returned it would bring back the transferred evil to the community. The question here is, can human guilt be effectively transferred to an animal? As evidenced by the events of history and every passing day, the scapegoat ritual has completely failed to rid humankind of evil. Just as the scapegoat ritual failed to remove sin or evil, so the death of Jesus failed to remove evil from the earth, and the evil of the supernatural dimension as hell supposedly continues to exist. Exorcisms continue to be performed to cast out devils, demons, and evil spirits. Daily earthly temptation by Satan or the Devil continues to be a topic of Baptist Sunday sermons.

The death of Jesus was based on the tradition of child sacrifice. Passages in the Torah show evidence of a long tradition of child sacrifice. These include the story of Abraham and Isaac in Genesis 22. Exodus 22:29-30 also shows evidence of a transition from child to animal sacrifice. "Thou shalt not delay to offer the first of thy ripe fruits, and of thy liquors: the firstborn of thy sons shalt thou give unto me. Likewise shalt thou do with thine oxen, and with thy sheep: seven days it shall be with his dam; on the eighth day thou shalt give it to me." The blood-thirsty god needed nourishment.

The god required three types of offerings. The first is the burnt offering, where the animal part was burned and the essence and flavor ascended to the god in the sky. The second is the thanks offering, in which part of the animal, the chest and shoulder was given to the priests.

There was also a sin offering, when the blood of an animal was sprinkled around the altar. With the sin offering, the male individual placed his hands on the animal's head and his sins were transferred to the substitute cow, sheep, goat or lamb of both sexes. But can guilt seriously be transferred from a human to an animal? In modern times these kinds of thinking and behaviors are considered deranged.

To believe is to be convinced, or to accept a particular view as true. To have faith is to trust in a particular view. The Catholic statement of belief and faith reads:

"We believe in one God, the Father, the Almighty, maker of heaven and earth, and of all that is seen and unseen. We believe in one Lord, Jesus Christ, the only Son of God, eternally begotten of the Father, God of God, Light of Light, true God from true God, begotten, not made, one in being with the Father. Through Him all things were made. For us men and for our salvation He came down from heaven: by the power of the Holy Spirit He was born of the Virgin Mary, and was made man. For our sake He was crucified under Pontius Pilate; He suffered, died, and was buried. On the third day He rose again according to the Scriptures; He ascended into heaven and is seated on the right hand of the Father. He will come again in glory to judge the living and the dead, and His kingdom shall have no end. We believe in the Holy Spirit, the Lord, the giver of life, who proceeds from the Father and the Son. With the Father and the Son He is worshipped and glorified. He has spoken through the prophets. We believe in one holy catholic and apostolic Church. We acknowledge one baptism for the forgiveness of sins. We look for the resurrection of the dead, and the life of the world to come. Amen."

The catechism and statement of faith of the Roman Catholic Church is that there is a human-like god who is also an all-powerful father and maker of all things. He had only one son, Jesus, who was begotten and not made or created, and Jesus is one with his father by which he is fully god, and he was born of Mary so is fully human. Crazy stuff but being fully god and fully human is a tenet of blind faith and not the findings of the modern science of genetics.

The evidence for being a god was based partly on the behaviors of Jesus; he taught and prophesized, did miracles and was physically resurrected, all of which are idealized as god-like. Being fully male human was based at least on his body functions; he got tired, hungry, and experienced fear and pain. Though not mentioned, being fully a profane human, he also had to perspire, urinate and defecate, fart and burp, had bad breath on occasion, and being fully male also had to have a penis and testicles, gotten erections, and even had sex.

Jesus preexisted in heaven and came down to earth for the salvation of humans. He was born of a virgin, Mary, who scholars of that era of history say would have been fourteen years old at the time of puberty and marriage. Jesus was most likely born in Bethlehem of Galilee just a short way from Nazareth, not the traditional Bethlehem of Judah located six miles south of Jerusalem. Life came from a male holy spirit referred to as "He," that comes from both the god and Jesus. The hope of a physical resurrection is the human deluded desire to exist again in the same physical form. There is also the view of a world to come, either a renewed earth and/or heavenly world.

Comments

The religion of Judaism relied on the commandments and so resulted in a legalism. Jesus reduced the number of commandments from 613 to three; "Love God with all your heart," and "your neighbor as your self" (Matthew 22:37; Mark 12:30-31; Luke 10:27) and "love one's enemies." (Matthew 5:44; Luke 6:27, 35) The individual is commanded to love by Jesus; "These things I command you, that ye love one another." (John15:17) The experience of love should be of importance, but nowhere in the book of Genesis and the beginning of existence is there a mention of love by the god.

There are only a few mentions of the word love in the entire book of Genesis; of Isaac's love of savory meat in 27:4, and 29:20, 32 referring to the love of Jacob and his wife Rachel. In the Exodus commandments, love is not mentioned, only honor, as in honoring of one's father and mother; one can assume love in this instance.

In Deuteronomy there are two imperatives to love God; "And thou shalt love the Lord thy God with all thine heart, and with all thy soul, and with all thy might." (Deuteronomy 6:5 and 30:6) In addition, there is one mention of love for strangers (Deuteronomy 10:19). In Leviticus, there is one mention of the love of one's neighbor. (19:18, 34)

While the god will punish some humans for their evil on earth, he usually waits until after physical death when they are closer to his presence in a supernatural dimension. He then judges and sends an individual to either heaven, hell, and perhaps purgatory. In the Middle East religions of Judaism, Christianity and Islam, since the god is the human-like origin of all that is good in life, Satan is the human-like origin of evil, pain, and suffering, the stooge of the good human-like god. Satan, Devil, or Lucifer is a human way of removing and separating evil from the goodness of the god. Yet in the following verses it is evident the extent of the god's capacity to create and to inflict evil; "I form the light, and create darkness: I make peace, and create evil: I the Lord do all these things." (Isaiah 45:7) "Therefore it shall come to pass, that as all good things are come upon you, which the Lord your God promised you; so shall the Lord bring upon you all evil things." (Joshua 23:15) "Then God sent an evil spirit." (Judges 9:23) "...therefore hath the Lord brought upon them all this evil." (1 Kings 9:9)

To be a Christian is to hold the view there is a human-like god who has a god-like human son. To associate with others while wearing nice clothes on Sunday shows that one is higher-like, not lower-like as in being poor, unkempt, and unclean. True kindness and love is rare while much hypocrisy is prevalent, and the public show ever continues.

## Chapter 7

*The religions of man each prevail,*
*Until one comes to triumph and the other fail;*
*Ah, the lonesome world;*
*Always wants to hear the latest fairy tale."*
    Al Ma'arri

### Islam

Roots of the religion of Islam can be found in pre-Islamic views and practices. Hubal was the pre-Islamic moon god and was worshipped at the water-well location of the Kaaba in Mecca, Saudi Arabia. The name Hubal may be derived from the Arabic suffix "hu," meaning he, and also taken to mean, nearest and ultimate, and "baal" meaning, lord. At night, especially during the rising of a full desert moon, its presence does appear to be much closer than any other heavenly body to the earth, and so worthy of worship.

Along with the ruling presence of the moon god Hubal, the shrine of the Kaaba also contained 360 other idols, perhaps representing the days of a lunar year, today calculated more accurately to be 354.34 days. Hubal was represented by a sculpture in human form made of carnelian, a brownish red semi-precious gemstone, or of red agate. Circumambulation was performed to Hubal, just as the ritual continues to be practiced today during the Hajj, the Islamic pilgrimage to worship the god Allah at Mecca. Divination was conducted in the presence of the idol with the use of seven arrows, and was in some way related to nocturnal dreams. Animal and blood offerings were also performed. The right hand of the sculpture is said to have been made of gold, perhaps associated with the golden color of the full moon.

When Muhammad, the founder of Islam, returned to conquer Mecca in the year 630 CE, he destroyed the sculpture of Hubal and the other idols in the Kaaba. But the influence of the moon-god in one way or another continues to the present day.

There may be a direct connection with the moon god Hubal and flags bearing the crescent moon shape and a star that may represent the planet Venus. The crescent moon and star symbol date from the 1300's CE, and today adorn the dome of many mosques and flags as the symbol of Islam.

The visible idol of Hubal was controlled by the ruling clan of Mecca and access to the god was limited. Jews and Christians lived in the trade town of Mecca and worshipped a non-visible god. The god of the Jews and Christians was not visible and was not controlled. Muhammad, the Meccan founder of Islam, aligned himself with the nonlocal and non-controlled yet still humanlike, Jewish and Christian god. The Christian god also had an afterlife reward as well.

Muhammad's revelation that founded the religion of Islam was a change from human-like sculptures of the sun, moon, and planet Venus, to the unseen human-like god Allah. This accomplishment was for the purpose of imposing social order and equality, and therefore the message of Allah reigning equally over all, appealed to the masses. Not a human-like image of the moon or planet Venus, but a greater unseen personality was needed to impose human order. The five times a day prayer in Islamic culture is symptomatic of the deeply felt need for a long searched for social order.

Muhammad

Muhammad (circa 570-632 CE) was the founder of the religion of Islam. Concerned about his Arabian society at the time, he decided that if the leaders of a culture would not politically improve social conditions, then the only other way to do so is to convince others to become followers of a single god. In this way, social changes occur through combined group agreement and effort. The god Allah is a model that provides an answer to the mystery of where things come from, how to live life, and what happens when death occurs. Agreeing each individual answers to one god in life and death, is a symbolic way of providing for social equality, since all are related to the god.

The religion of what is today called Islam was first known as Muhammadism, referring to the poet-prophet who recited his inspired words of the Quran. While there are many conflicting passages, anyone who listens to some of the beautiful inspired language of the Quran, cannot help but to be touched by feelings that some of the words evoke. The words of the Quran, like other theistic writings, are the result of the human strain and struggle to rise above the human condition. To rise above the human condition in the theistic tradition requires the psychological maneuver of being called by and rising toward a human-like greater god.

The Quran is a poetic work. Those who listened to and followed Muhammad soon began to accept, on his insistence, that they were not following and submitting to the teachings of Muhammad but were submitting to the human-like god, Allah. The religion of Islam is really the shadow of this one man and his early supporters who he managed to convince, that he was uttering the god or angel inspired words of the Quran.

While the ego of Muhammad was deemphasized, the insistence on the ego of a human-like god was over emphasized. In the words of the Quran, the god Allah is the ultimate all-knowing, all-powerful ego. There is a saying in Islam; Insha Allah, meaning "if god wills." Muslims see good fortune, as well as the suffering of accidents, illness, and death as willed by the god. All things and events are also predestined by the god. The great size of the sky and earth and its endless rhythms of time reduce the significance of human life to miniscule significance. Seeking some personal importance serves to evoke humans to magnify human attributes to the greater human-like god Allah.

"All that is in the heavens and the earth magnifies Allah; He is the All-mighty, the All-wise. To Him belongs the Kingdom of the heavens and the earth; He gives life, and He makes to die, and He is powerful over everything." (Surah 57:1-2) "Say: Nothing will happen to us except what Allah has decreed for us: He is our protector: and on Allah let the believers put their trust." (Surah 9:51) "Do you wish to guide him whom Allah has caused to err? And whomsoever Allah causes to err, you shall by no means find a way for him." (Surah 4:88)

During the changes of life experience, in order to counteract the chance of accident and illness, every individual seeks stability, comprehension and knowledge. Unable to find stability, enough comprehension and reliable knowledge, individuals turn to a conception, the conceived safe haven of a human-like god. For Muslims the deity is Allah. The concept of a god was conceived by humans for humans. A human-like god is the human explanation of how the environment and life came into existence, how humans should live life, and what awaits humans after death. Looking at the blatant evidence for the suffering of human existence, it is a strain to hold to this view of a human-like god. But the lone individual view is bolstered by the religious group as a whole, and there is strength en masse.

The anthropomorphic religions of the Middle East are not cognitively advanced. The religions of the Jews, Christians, and Muslims, have always contributed to conflict and war. Any religion that relies on the ego of a human-like god as a reality has only a capacity for conceived belief, not for reliable perceived knowledge. Imagining the greater ego of a god as wanting and sanctioning humans to kill as the will of the god to get his way, is a serious cognitive impairment. It is more certain that the desire to kill in war is a willful desire conditioned by excess testosterone levels of human male egos. In every country, those who fight wars are males, the prison population consists mainly of males, and so it seems human males are the problem on planet earth.

Just as with Judaism, there is no emphasis or method of connection with the origin of existence, only ritual submission to the commandment laws or to the willing of the omnipotent male god. Influenced by Hindu and Buddhist philosophy, Islamic mystics known as Sufis do seek "fana," the removing of ignorance of the ego, to reveal a glimpse of the potential inside. Sufis prefer not to worship the ego of a human-like god through empty repetitive religious rituals. The traditional Muslim worshiper, who submits or surrenders, does so mainly to meet the ritual requirements of Islam. In traditional Islam there is no surrender to the aesthetic sensing of an inside connection with the outside origin of existence.

A religious view is a fixed idea, and is reinforced by repetition of thoughts, emotions, and accepted behaviors. The fixation on a god ego is the human longing for an organized, stable, and intelligent authority. Humans look to a god for protection from the suffering of biological life, and protection from the potential of future suffering during an afterlife. The origin of things is not a supernatural intelligence. This is not to deny a supernatural dimension, only that no human-like god intelligence is the origin of it. The origin of things is a blind, generating ever-active force. This is quite evident in the surplus of living forms that are daily produced, and of which only a fraction survive. When considered, even the human necessity of eating other life forms is distressing. What kind of intelligence would bring forth the excess of life only to be consumed? The generating activity of forms does not need the intelligence or concern of a human-like god. That which is present as a generating and transforming function does not need an outside agent. A human-like god represents only human concern for humans.

In the Quran, the poet Muhammad directs the attention of faithful followers externally to a human-like god as the origin of existence. His words also seek to foster agreement among adherents as to the acceptance of his poetically inspired views. Over time there developed an obsession for social structure and adherence to the rituals of the Five Pillars of Islam.

A Muslim is one who submits or surrenders his or her will to the god Allah. Muhammad insisted upon individual submission to please a distant human-like god. In reality, submission was to human leaders who promoted what they deemed as good, such as peace and harmony to fellow humans. A greater god is the conceived symbol for the greater good of social harmony. A human-like god has never appeared on the scene to impose social order on his own. There is only human interpretation of events, not as a cause and effect process of life, but as some kind of reward, punishment, or plan by the god Allah.

The ritual behavior of religion is a shared practice of seeking agreement among the participants. Agreement can then conduce to harmony and cooperation.

This can be thrown off kilter by an unexpected event, such as the split of Islam into Sunni and Shia sects over differences in the succession of leaders. The split in Islam occurred when Muhammad chose his father-in-law, Abu Bakr, as his successor rather than his cousin and son-in-law Ali. Obviously, the ego of the god Allah or the ego of an angel did not step forward to resolve the conflict situation. This was left for the egos of humans to resolve, and of course there followed much bloodshed.

The prophet Muhammad died on June 8, 632 CE. The Arabic word caliph, means, successor, and is a title that refers to political and religious leaders who succeeded Muhammad. The first caliph was Muhammad's father-in-law, Abu Bakr, who was the father of his favorite wife, Aisha, and in whose arms Muhammad is said to have died. Abu Bakr was caliph for only two years when he died of natural causes or was poisoned. Before dying in 634 CE, he named Umar (also a father-in-law of Muhammad) as the second caliph. In 644 Omar was stabbed six times while in the Medina mosque at prayer, and died three days later. The third caliph was Uthman, a son-in-law of Muhammad. He is remembered for compiling the Quran. He was killed at home in 656 CE, and as his wife sought to defend him, some fingers were cut from her hand. Ali was a cousin of Muhammad and the husband of Muhammad's daughter Fatima. He became the fourth caliph who ruled from 656 to 661 CE. Ali was assassinated with a poisonous sword during prayer and died two days later.

The problem of succession was a dynamic of combining both a theological and a political system. This dual dynamic of the ego of a god and egoism of human politics certainly contributed to a deadly brew of conflict and wars within the religion. Islam eventually split into two groups, the Sunni who followed the caliphs, and the Shia or Shi'ite who favored the view that Ali was the proper successor to Muhammad. The Shia would only follow leaders descended from Ali.

Sunnis are the eighty-five percent majority of world Muslims, The majority of the population of Iran practices the Shia form of Islam which makes up about twelve percent of world Muslims, or about 140 million. About forty percent of this number live in Iran.

## Sufism

Traditional Islam does not care for the Sufi sect of religious orders. This is so as faith, belief, and ritual behavior are more important for traditional Islam than Sufi practice. For the average Muslim, the self-exploration and discipline of meditation takes too much time from worldly pursuits. The practice of meditation also requires too much effort. Traditional theistic religion, not only Islam, is for the unintelligent and lazy which the vast majority of humankind are.

The origin of Sufism can be traced to the 800's CE as a response to increasing religious dogmatism and the political emphasis in the practice of Islam. Sufism was a reaction to the teachings derived from a distant anthropomorphic god, who was only interested in having humans follow his dictates in the Quran. Sufis were also influenced by the more experiential Eastern religions of Hinduism and Buddhism. The following three verses were written by the Sufi poet Jalal al Rumi (1207-1275 CE).

"What dwells in the rose that made it open, dwells also here in my chest."

"Seek always to comprehend a way to the sacred,
Seeking the ways of the world is a slow sickness."

"Hangovers come with love, yet love is the cure for hangovers."

As seen in these Sufi poems, the way to personal transcendent experience is to reduce one's ego of self-importance, and to become aware of a shared greater origin of existence. Sufism is the seeing past egos, of oneself, others, and even the ego of a human-like god. The inspired words of the poet-prophet Muhammad emphasized social structure and equality. In contrast, the words of the poet-prophet Rumi emphasize aesthetic individual discovery and development.

## Ego

The individual ego is more likely to pay heed to a greater ego, even though imaginary, and so treat his fellow egos with more respect and care. Recognizing a greater unlimited ego of a human-like god is a way of getting out of one's own limited ego. Recognizing a greater ego who rewards and punishes the smaller human ego, is a way of getting beyond the confines of individual ego,

In theistic thinking, one gets beyond individual ego only by recognizing a greater ego. Yet while the sense of individual ego is reduced, depending on individual conscience of right or wrong, the ego remains intact. The psychological step of conversion to recognizing an imaginary greater ego is only partially effective. The human ego remains intact and egocentrically continues to seek reward and avoid punishment. No observational and psychological discipline is developed or applied, such as meditation or analysis of self. Only the Indian body and mind disciplines of yoga, meditation, and asceticism, seek to effectively reduce and remove the ego structure.

Recognizing a shared god-ego also makes the social environment safer by transcending individual differences. While having a greater unlimited ego in charge, one can relax one's own egocentric struggle with the individual egos of family, friends, and fellow humans. A greater ego will take care of any evil egos in this very life, or in an afterlife of hells.

A human-like god ego is merely the human ego to prevail in life and an afterlife. If performed for a greater ego of a god by groups of lesser human egos, great violence is also justified. Hence the medieval Crusades, Inquisitions, armed struggles to the death in the so-called yet misnamed Holy Land, and fatwas and jihads.

## Chapter 8

*Through many a long life his discrimination ripens: He seeks refuge in the knowledge that Brahman is all. How rare are such great ones!*
*Bhagavad Gita*

### Hinduism

### Teacher

The Hindu name Amiya means, nectar and delight. The man I am referring to was born and grew up in the area of India known as West Bengal. In stature he was about five-feet six inches tall, thin, with a light brown complexion, and had dark brown eyes that emanated a gentle intensity and calmness. It was my good fortune and karma to interact with him over the course of two years.

In the spring month of March of the year 1973, Dr. Amiya Chakravarty (1901-1986) unexpectedly became my guru, my spiritual teacher. I remember vividly one day in the early spring of the year, when I and a few others met with him in a philosophy class on the New Paltz campus of the State University of New York. Listening to him speak, I closed my eyes to feel the warm sun shining through the window on my face. I soon opened my eyes and Amiya was gazing directly at me. He then slowly turned his head to the right and then resumed looking straight at me. My attention was drawn to his dark shining eyes, and as I was doing so I felt a palpable magnetic aura emanating from his presence. My thoughts rapidly increased in an attempt to comprehend what was happening. As I focused more on his eyes, I became aware that they were very dark and that his pupils were dilated almost to the edge of the iris.

I sat transfixed staring, and felt a magnetic energy between us, and the experience of somehow entering his eyes. I felt as if I, or my consciousness, had entered the opening of a tunnel and was moving through vast space, when suddenly I began to experience a feeling of total love…a love I had never known before.

I became aware of a soft pulsing in my forehead, throat, and chest area. This magnetic feeling permeated me until the distinctness of the personal identity of my body and mind faded into a vision of unity with, I can only say, the cosmic mystery of existence.

It was an experience of the capacity of love within me being awakened and simultaneously being totally loved by another. I felt or sensed the stillness of eternity but slowly moments of time returned and I actually felt an engagement with the passing seconds. Subjectively, I felt the experience had lasted for ten minutes or so but in reality no more than two or three minutes had elapsed. Slowly Amiya again turned his head to the right and then looked straight ahead to glance at others, and then back to me. I sat in a condition of surprise and mild shock. Whatever had just transpired was now definitely over.

When class was dismissed, mildly dazed I quickly located my two friends to share my unusual experience with them. I later found out that the experience was what is known in Hindu tradition as "shaktipat." Shakti is energy and pata means to touch. Shaktipat is given by a guru to a student who he thinks is ready or deserving to experience spiritual awakening. The experience that fateful day was blissful oneness and wholly otherworldly. I honestly do not know what Dr. Amiya Chakravarty saw in me personally to bestow the blessing of shaktipat upon me that warm spring day in the year 1973. I have been grateful ever since, and reverberations continue to echo through my life due to those blissful moments he so generously bestowed upon me. Over the course of two years spent in various classes with Amiya, I gleaned the following insightful views on Hinduism.

Knowledge of Hinduism

Like most cultures who came up with an answer to the metaphysical origin of existence, Hindus were biased by human attributes, and projected a human-like intelligence to be the cause of existence. Most Hindus attribute the origin of the environment and life to the intelligence of a god that formed things from the outside, like humans form a clay pot.

Folk religion for the masses found this view easy to accept, as it did not require much of an effort to think. This popular erroneous way of thinking could not and did not, consider the energy within a living form to come from the environment, and in turn is a continuation of a cosmic force.

Like other cultures, Hindus relied on anthropomorphism to comprehend the origin of existence. While there are many human-like gods and goddesses in Hindu popular religion, the main deities are Brahma, Vishnu, and Shiva, symbols for reality processes.

Brahma symbolizes the coming into existence of relative temporal events and forms. Brahma is the creator god and is portrayed in human-like form, although usually with four arms and four faces, symbolic of omnipresent creativity in all of the four directions.

It was observed that there was a balance and an order in existence, so Vishnu in human-like form symbolizes balance and order; he is the preserver. There are cause and effect laws of order and continuity as a cyclic change of day and night, the seasons and the weather. There is a homeostasis function within living forms. Things exist and are preserved for varying lengths of time.

Shiva is the human-like god that represents the observation that all formations change and eventually go out of existence. He is the destroyer, and is also associated with sexuality and the bringing forth of life that ends in the experience of death. The association of Shiva, the god of death and destruction, with reproduction, as exemplified in the lingam-yoni (sculpture of male and female organs) is recognition of the antecedent of human demise, which is sexuality and reproduction.

There is an old riddle, "Which came first, the chicken or the egg?" No matter how you look at this circular question, you cannot have one without the other. To have a chicken, you have to have an egg, but it had to have been laid by a chicken. The traditional answer of folk religion is that a human-like god intelligence first made a chicken and its egg-laying capacity at a distant point in time, and this is how the life cycle of poultry got started.

What is primary is force and energy, not human-like god intelligence. A theist who accepts the view of a human-like god would remark, "Where did the force and energy come from? It has to come from somewhere and it has to have a maker. It just cannot come from nothing." Contrary to unthinking popular view, there can be no human awareness of force or energy having either a beginning or an ending, only a transformation and relative function. In contrast, in every culture the god or goddess has an origin in time. Every deity has come about in the historical process via humans in differing cultures.

The Hindu word "tapas" means heat-energy, and is the primal origin of all environmental and living forms and functions. As such tapas is not dependent on human story-telling but only on discovery and observation. An inexhaustible nonhuman cosmic force beyond space and time, not intelligence, continues to generate and resupply the outer and inner energy requirement of all environmental and living forms. Intelligence arrived late on the scene with animals and humans. Its long precursor of intelligence was, and continues to be, energy. It is quite easy to see that intelligence for the human species has only recently evolved. Evolved human intelligence produces advances in knowledge, yet present levels of knowledge continue to be frequently erroneous and contain unforeseen consequences.

The unknown cause events is made known through the insertion of a symbol, a human conceived god as a beginning in a beginningless and endless time. A human-like god is not based on perception but is based on conception generated through imagination and rudimentary reasoning. A god or goddess is a finite mooring on an infinite sea of space and unlimited time. Not to maintain this mooring would produce fear and despair when looking and thinking about the vast unknown cosmos, and one's individual vulnerable relationship with it.

Brahman

India, with its problems of over-crowding, poverty, and caste differences, is the most spiritual and aesthetically sensitive culture on the earth. What other culture can possibly claim this, or even be second to India?

An astounding cognitive leap occurred in India circa 700 BCE. Through the practice of meditation and ascetic yoga disciplines, a minority of Hindu seers brought an end to the many human-like gods and goddesses. They arrived at the view of a metaphysical origin that was not human-like. The seers gave the name Brahman to this cosmic presence. It was an aesthetic discovery of nonhuman-like energy and the relative presence of it within the individual, they called atma. The term atma is usually translated into English as meaning, soul or spirit.

The Upanishads are a collection of Hindu spiritual teachings of a guru (Sanskrit gu, meaning dark, and ru, meaning light), a teacher who brings light to remove the dark ignorance of a student. The oldest of these teachings originated circa 800-700 BCE. There are a number of Upanishads but only fourteen are considered important. The Upanishads speak of an unseen origin given the name Brahman, derived from the Sanskrit word brih, meaning, to expand. For Hindus there is an expanding unseen presence that brought forth the environment and living forms through movement and growth. The question is, what is it and where is it?

The Taittiriya Upanishad remarks, "In the beginning all this was nonexistent. From it was born what exists." In these few simple words, there is no mention of the personality of a god at the beginning, but rather the presence of "it," the origin from which has come the immanent force within the functions and the forms of existence.

The Mundaka Upanishad makes use of analogy to say, "As, from the blazing fire, sparks essentially akin to it fly forth by the thousand, so also, my good friend, do various beings come forth from the imperishable Brahman and...again return." It is further said, "By attaining higher knowledge the wise behold everywhere Brahman, which cannot be seen or held, which has no cause or attribute, no eyes or ears, no hands or feet; is eternal and omnipresent, pervading all and extremely subtle; which is imperishable and the origin of all beings."

The Mundaka Upanishad states, "Brahman is not grasped by the eye, nor by speech, nor by the other senses, nor by penance or good works. A man becomes pure through serenity of intellect; thereupon, in meditation, he beholds the one that is without parts."

The Svetasvatara Upanishad teaches Brahman has entered into all forms. "The luminous One, who is in fire, who is in water, who has entered into the whole world, who is in plants, who is in trees; to that one let there be adoration! Yea, let there be adoration!" While Brahman as a cosmic force is difficult to comprehend, it is possible to observe the effects and functions of it. Brahman is the origin and support of all nonliving and living forms.

The Katha Upanishad says, "If a man is able to realize Brahman here, before the falling asunder of his body, then he is liberated; if not, he is embodied again in the created worlds." If an individual reduces his many cloying desires for life, the cycle of reincarnation will be brought to end.

Only a few discerning individuals in a very few older cultures did not anthropomorphize the origin of the environment and living forms. Instead, they relied on close observation and perception of what is outside and what is inside. Aside from the Hindu view of Brahman, only the early philosophy of Buddhism, the Chinese philosophical view of the Tao, and a Greek philosopher by the name of Heraclitus, managed to excel in the impressive cognitive achievement of not indulging in the imagining of human-like gods.

Yoga

Yoga literally means yoke. The practice consists of various mental, physical, and ethical disciplines to find the yoke, the connection within. Individual practice enhances comprehension of how the individual is connected to the environment and to a subtle unseen metaphysical origin. There is also samsara, the round of birth and death, until the effort of yoga reduces this karma process.

The following words pertaining to the origin of existence were said at a Hindu Vedanta religious service by Swami Pavitrananada in New York City.

"That from which the whole universe has come into being, that to which we owe the existence of our bodies and minds, let us strive to know that and that alone; it is the way to bliss, it is the way to immortality."

The discipline of yoga relies on gradual ethical, physical, and meditative training. Attention is focused, directed, and utilized to better comprehend that all forms are relative to a single cosmic force that divides into multiple forms of existence. From the primal force of Brahman, there was a traction, a pulling apart as a division, to become a divine process of vining as a growing of energy elements, environment, and dependent living forms. All forms are a divine going and growing from a primal force. The practice of yoga recognizes the reality of a primal origin of shared force and energy, as seen through the eyes of aesthetic sensitivity and compassion. The practice of yoga contributes to ethical purity that is often palpably sensed not only by humans but animals as well.

There is a strong ethical component to the many practices of yoga as there is a recognition of karma, the one law of cause and effect. There are said to be Hindu hells, but it is individual karma which causes this devolved effect. The cosmic force of Brahman is not human-like and does not judge or punish. Only the cause and effect law of karma metes out a just existence. Events happen according to cause and effect, not the result of an anthropomorphic god. Just as there is no ultimate beginning, there is no ending of a final judgment. Beginning and ending and judgment are always in the present moment, rapidly appearing and disappearing in the human brain.

It may be theorized that the view of reincarnation was developed by observing cyclical events in the environment. The view may also have been generated by a desire of the living for the deceased to come back to life. It may also be the result of a desire by the dying to avoid oblivion and to continue to live.

Karma includes behaviors, desires, emotions, and thoughts. Karma, the cause and effect law of motion and momentum, is what propels all in transforming circles of existence. Hindus think there is both, a species and individual evolution on earth, and an evolution in an afterlife.

There are various heavens and hells into which one can be born and evolve or devolve; to eventually die and reincarnate in recurring cycles.

Modern western philosophy agrees with the view of karma, and this is what is referred to as the theory of soft determinism. The theory advocates that all events, from subatomic particles to galaxies, are strictly determined by a single cause and effect process. However, there is some small room for freedom. If an individual is aware of cause and effect, then he can utilize the law to get to where he would like to be in life. Hindu philosophy preceded this contemporary view, and is in complete agreement with it.

## Chapter 9

*At birth we come, at death we go, bearing nothing.*
*Chinese Proverb*

### Taoism

Lao Tzu lived circa 550 BCE in China, and is reputed to have written at least some of the approximate 5,000 words of the Tao Te Ching. Not much is known of his life, except that he may have been a keeper of books and records for a local ruler. Legend reports that Lao Tzu came to dislike court life and the inability and failure of humans to behave ethically.

Chinese pictograms or ideograms are difficult to translate. Word meanings have also changed through the centuries. English translations of the Tao Te Ching vary so much that when reading various versions, it is difficult to recognize that it is the same written work.

The oldest known pictogram of the Chinese word Tao, consists of three images that include; tufts of hair atop the human head of a group leader, and symbols for feet both moving and standing still. The pictogram suggests a ruling and therefore an organizing and originating presence having the attributes of movement and stillness. Though the Chinese did not anthropomorphize human-like gods as did other less cognitively astute cultures, they utilize a human figure in the pictogram for a non-human-like cosmic force from which all things come into existence.

The word Tao has been most often translated into English as meaning, Way. The pictogram for the word te, consists of three figures that suggest movement, straight, and heart, and can best be translated as meaning, true. The Chinese word ching, long ago referred to pictograms written on bamboo strips and tied together to make a roll. This today is what would be called a book. The Chinese title of Tao Te Ching, means most accurately in English, a book for the true knowing of the way things are.

## Yin Yang

Yin-yang is a symbol of Taoism, and mention of it in the early literature dates from circa 700-500 BCE. The word yin means, shade or shadow, and yang means, bright or light. The symbol originated from observation of the changing ratio of shadow and light occurring on the side of a hill from morning to evening. This process was observed to be dualistic yet interrelated and complimentary, not opposing or antagonistic.

In Chinese thinking, the circumference of the circle symbolizes Tao and also symbolizes "chi or qi" meaning, universal energy. In popular thinking, the dark yin side is associated with the feminine, yielding, earth, and bland foods, while the light yang side is associated with the masculine, force, heaven, and spicy foods.

In the Taoist view, the outer circumference of the yin-yang shape, symbolizes the Tao as the greater origin of relative forces and energies of existence. The sphere consists of a dark and a light droplet shape that symbolically suggest the flow from the unseen to the seen in changing recurring cycles. The Tao as an unseen force and origin of relative motion is suggested by the dark half of the symbol, which expands to a limit, and from that cause or change begins the point of expansion of the light half. The two droplets also suggest the changing diurnal cycles of night and day, and the visible formations of the universe, including stars, sun, moon, planets, the earth environment, and living forms. Visible forms after a time expand to a limit of development, and then reach a point of change and return to the dark unseen causal force.

In some versions of the yin-yang symbol, there is a small white dot located in the dark droplet. The dot suggests how visible formations begin in, and come from, the causal cosmic force. In contrast, a dark dot in the white droplet suggests a symbol of the presence of the causal origin as an immanent unseen force within the seen formations of existence.

The yin-yang figure is symbolic of a cyclic flow of force, from an unseen causal origin to the various seen effects of relative formations.

Tao

Tao is the origin of existence and all things flow forth from it. All formations flow from a cosmic force into the soft and hard things of existence. Coming into existence does not occur as a hard or rigid process, but rather a flow of chi or qi, force and energy. All things flow from a subtle rarified presence into an existence of time.

Through observing the human body which is dependent upon, and derived from the environment, Taoism avoided the anthropomorphic ego of a god authority and commanded ethics. For example, it was observed that the environment consists of rock that is hard, soil that is soft, and flowing air and water. It was also observed that the human body consists of the hardness of bones, soft skin, muscle and organs, breathing of air and the flowing liquid of blood, urine, saliva, and tears. Psychologically and behaviorally, the individual must at times be hard, soft, or flowing. The exclusion, and under or over-emphasis of one quality results in an unnatural imbalance. An individual can be too hard or not hard enough, or too soft or not soft enough. For Taoism, as exemplified by the yin-yang symbol, ethics of right and good is a natural harmony of flowing.

Taoist sages observed the visible environment as a way of gaining knowledge of the invisible Tao. Since the way of heaven is unknown, and since a god did not appear to give instruction, the individual can find a cue of guidance of how to behave in the environment. The environment is primal to humans. This is evident, since humans are dependent on the environment and the environment is not dependent on humans. The environment is greater in size and longer lasting than humans, who live an average of seventy-five years.

From the Tao came the way or flow of chi or qi, the force and energy which brought the environment into existence. Taoists recognize reality as a place of formations consisting of the qualities of hardness, softness, and flowing.

Examples are hardness of stone, softness of soil, and flowing wind and water. While hard, soft, and flowing oppose each other, they are interdependent and come from the one cosmic force called Tao. With the support of the earth environment of stone, soil, and flow of water and air, living forms came into existence. Taoists also observed the qualities of hardness, softness, and flowing in living forms. Hardness is necessary for support of the soft soil and flowing water. Softness of the soil is necessary for plants to grow in. Living plants and trees have the hardness of support of stems, wood trunks and branches, while animals and humans have the hardness of bones. Plants and trees have softness of leaves while animals and humans have the softness of hair, muscles and skin. All living forms drink in, circulate, and respire flowing water and air, while animals and humans have circulating flow of urine and blood.

The Taoist observation of the three qualities of environment can be utilized as a general personality theory of behavior. Psychologically, the behavior of individuals in society can be hard, soft, or flowing. The individuals who are hard rely on aggression, such as governments that utilize a military, police who enforce laws and utilize punishment. Individuals who are soft rely on kindness, assistance, and work to reduce human suffering, such as doctors, psychologists and psychiatrists.

There are some members of society who rely on flowing; these are the aesthetic and spiritually oriented who seek wholeness and seek to experience oneness with the greater force of the relative flow of existence. These individuals seek to be, and are aware of the flow of passing seconds, so do not become attached to things or do not become an overly hard obstruction to others.

With flowing, one does not get stuck opposing or holding onto relative ideas or things. Like water and air, all is a flow of changing moments of time. It is all too easy to get lost in the excessive flow of thoughts and emotions. When these are calmed in meditation, then an increase in comprehension and clarity occurs. These few individuals, through meditation, reduce and calm the flow of memories, imaginations, emotions, and willing behaviors.

They are able to reach the origin of all relative change; the unseen and unlimited cosmic reservoir of the Tao.

Giving Mother

Tao is the name given to an unseen cosmic force that brings forth all things. While the Tao cannot be perceived directly, it can be intuitively known through observation of environmental and living forms. The intuitive verses of the Tao Te Ching were inspired through close observation and meditation on the natural environment. The Tao as the beginning of existence cannot be spoken of, or described through words. Only attributes of the Tao as observed in the many events and forms can be described. Based on observation of relative forms of existence, the Tao has three valuable attributes. These are giving, balance, and not wanting to be foremost.

67. The world says of Tao,
That it seems to be nothing.
It is because it is so vast
That it appears as nothing;
If it resembled anything,
It would long ago have ended.
It has three valuable attributes;
Giving,
Balance,
Not wanting to be foremost.
Giving, all things come from it;
Balanced it does not use all of itself,
And so retains its vastness;
Not wanting to go ahead of others,
It contains all.
Now if people forget about giving,
And are concerned only with getting;
If they do not have balance,
And live unbalanced;
If instead of not wanting to be foremost,
They always want to be foremost;
They shall soon meet with doom....

The Tao as primal force is so vast it cannot be perceived with the senses. In not wanting to be foremost, Tao remains the transcendent origin of things. Translated into English, the classical Chinese word "ci tsu" literally means, mother and connotes giving and yielding. Through giving birth there is a transition from the transcendent Tao into the immanent force of environmental and living forms. The unseen Tao gives and yields, it brings forth the stars, sun, moon, planets, and the earth environment from which come the many living forms. All things in existence are a giving of the Tao.

While the Tao does not have a human-like personality or gender, the living form which is most similar to it is the female or mother. The image of the female is prevalent throughout the verses of the Tao Te Ching. The Tao, the earth, and all mothers provide sustenance for what they bring forth.

1. Words cannot describe
The eternal Tao.
It is that from which
Both heaven and earth come.
It is the mother of life,
And all things here.
To glimpse this great source,
There must be one desire,
Just as when a variety of things are wanted,
There must be many desires.
The One and the many things,
Can be seen as the same,
And also as separate differences.
Each is difficult to comprehend,
The one source,
And the many things.
Yet by comprehending the latter,
The unseen gate of the former is reached.

The transcendent cosmic origin of existence, the Tao, cannot be described with words. The Tao can only be indirectly comprehended through observation of the phenomena that have come from it.

Though difficult to comprehend the Tao, there must be a focus of desire to do so. Through observation of the attributes of phenomena that come from the Tao, intuitive comprehension of it can be experienced.

2. Tao unseen,
Is the source of all that is seen,
Both hard and soft,
Large and small,
Sounds and silence,
Beginning and ending.
So the wise know both,
The great unseen,
And what has come from it....

Tao is the source of the opposites of existence. Yet these differing forms all share one immanent force that has come from the one unseen Tao.

14. One can call it elusive,
Since one may look but never see it,
Unseen like air one may listen but never hear it,
So subtle it cannot be held;
Lacking these three attributes,
It is difficult to comprehend.
Having no beginning that light can illuminate,
Having no end which darkness can obscure,
A presence difficult to name,
Unseen source of all things.
It is an unformed form,
A shapeless shape,
So any description of it is obscure.
Yet one can meet that which has no face,
And follow that which has no behind.
Aware of this primal Tao,
One can live well today,
True knowledge is to see the thread,
Connecting all things with the Tao.

25. A presence there is,
Which was before the
earth and sky;
Silent, shapeless,
mateless, unchanging.
Yet in bringing forth forms untiring,
It is the Mother of all.
Having no name,
I call it Tao....

The Tao is a silent shapeless, mate-less, and unchanging source, yet from which there is a transition into the relative force of environment and life forms. The Tao is the Mother of all things as it has given birth to the sun with which to see and to be warm. The Tao has given the earth for support, water to drink, and air to breathe; it has given plants and animals for food, and wood for fire. The Tao is always giving to sustain existence. The environmental form that most resembles the Tao is flowing water.

6. The valley spring never ceases to flow,
It is like an always giving mother.
The fount of the ever-giving Mother,
Is the root of heaven and earth,
Dimly seen, yet it is there;
Never ceasing to flow.

Lao Tzu exhorts the individual to cultivate the Tao's attribute of giving that he can only compare to the valley spring of unceasing fresh flowing water.

22. Soften and so not break,
Bend and then straighten.
Wise men of old have also said,
Soften and so not break,
Truly this can preserve us to the end.

To give way or be yielding and flexible contributes to well-being and happiness. Throughout human existence, there have been untold instances when a trifling disagreement has developed into harmful consequences for the individuals involved.

Tempers flare and violence and aggression is the result. In verse 76 it is pointed out that what is hard and unyielding soon meets with doom, while what is soft and yielding continues to live.

76. When alive man is flexible and soft,
In death he is stiff and hard.
Grass and trees when alive bend easily,
But when dead are dry and unbending.
What is hard and unbending belongs to death;
And what is supple and soft belongs to life.
Tough uncaring soldiers soon fall,
And a hardened tree falls to the axe.
What is hard and unyielding soon topples,
While the soft and yielding continues upright.

Lao Tzu uses the image of water to convince that the flowing and soft quality of water overcomes that which is resistant and hard.

78. There is nothing more soft
and flowing than water,
Yet when it moves over that which
is resistant and hard,
Nothing can change its course....

28. Know the male nature,
But keep to the role of female,
And so become a valley,
Through which the always true can flow.

The verses suggest that human knowing and willing behavior should resemble water and that like water should flow conforming to limitations of the environment. Like water, thoughts should remain fluid and not become hard or an obstacle.

Balance

The second attribute of the Tao is the Chinese word chien, meaning balance, as in not going to extremes. The Tao imbues and imparts a balance to the relative functions of the environment and living forms.

There is a balance of night and day, summer and winter, rain and drought. For living forms there is a natural balance of waking and sleeping, eating and drinking, excretory functions, activity and rest, and health and illness.

43. That which is most yielding in the world,
Flows easily over the hardest.
That which has no firm structure,
Penetrates that which has no crevice.
This is why I know the benefit
Of not resorting to force.
That which teaches without words,
And the benefit of not using force,
These things few in the world comprehend.

46. The greatest vice is to have many desires,
There is no greater fault than to be discontent,
There is no greater harm than being possessive;
Being content is to always have enough.

Not Wanting To Be Foremost

The third attribute of the Tao is the Chinese phrase, bugan wei tianxia xian, meaning, not wanting to be foremost.

67. The world says of Tao,
That it seems to be nothing.
It is because it is so vast,
That it appears as nothing.
If it resembled anything,
It would long ago have ended....

66. The river and sea become great bodies of water,
By taking the lower position....

8. The highest man like water,
Benefits all, refusing none,
While occupying a lower place,
And so is like the Tao....

Verse 67 mentions the Tao appears as nothing, and there is no need to be foremost. Verse 66 is an example of the environment not wanting to be foremost. Verse 8 mentions the attribute of not wanting to be foremost concerning human behavior. Like water, the wise person benefits all, without wanting to occupy a higher place or wishing to be recognized as superior or foremost in any way, and therefore is in accord with the Tao.

Lao Tzu says that humans should emulate the behavior of the Tao in daily life. The Tao, as the source of all things, exhibits the attributes of giving, balance, and not wanting to be foremost. The individual is admonished and encouraged to develop these attributes or qualities through behaviors. One should be just as concerned with giving as with getting. There should be a balance in the areas of living, including work, physical and mental health, nutrition, family, and social relationships. With balance, the individual can properly appreciate human existence and not be so concerned with one's own inflated ego. Without balance, the individual often seeks to be foremost, regardless of the limitation and suffering it imposes on one's self and others.

Nature puts all environmental and living things where it wants them. All things are ever moved by relative forces and energies, in turn moved by a single cosmic force. Modern cosmology has reached its terminus of observation and measurement of phenomena by comprehending the presence of dark energy that moves galaxies, and dark matter that forms and holds the galaxies and visible universe together. These modern views are quite similar to the older Chinese commentarial wisdom of Taoism.

Edward Conklin

## Chapter 10

*Not to be born is best, when all is reckoned in. The next best by far, when one has been born is to go back quickly as possible from where one came. Sophocles*

## Heraclitus

While Socrates, Plato, and Aristotle are the most recognized of the Greek philosophers, the wisest was one by the name of Heraclitus. He lived circa 540-475 BCE in the Ionian Greek town of Ephesus, today located on the coast of Turkey.

Heraclitus recorded his philosophical observations in aphorisms, short pithy sayings that were handed down and quoted accurately, and some probably inaccurately by other philosophers through the years. Approximately 124 aphorisms that were more or less attributed to Heraclitus have survived through the years, and have been collected and grouped together in differing arrangements by various scholars.

Heraclitus had an interest in the comprehension of what he referred to as the Logos. By Logos, Heraclitus meant, one cosmic force, immanently within all things, including the environment and living forms. The individual could become aware of the Logos by observation and contemplation of what move nature and living forms. For example, he said:

"Wisdom is to know the one which moves all things."

"Heeding not me but the Logos, wisdom sees all things are one."

"Though the Logos eternally exists, humans have no knowledge of it."

"Though all things come from the Logos, few comprehend it."

"The Logos is day and night, winter and summer, war and peace, fullness and hunger; it takes differing shapes, just as fire mingled with various incense is named as different odors."

"It separates and brings together; it moves and rests."

"See as joined, whole and parts, attraction and opposition, similarity and differences. The one indwells the many, and all comes from the one."

Heraclitus says in these aphorisms that the Logos is eternally and immanently present, and that all things have come from this single cosmic force. Most humans fail to discern the one force immanent in differing forms and functions, and therefore do not comprehend it. There is a duality of form and parts, differences of attraction and opposition, sameness and dissimilarity, yet they are joined by one external force immanently shared that connects all things together. Humans are deceived in their knowledge of reality as can be seen in this amusing aphorism.

"Humans are deceived in their knowledge of things that exist; even as was the wisest of Greeks, Homer. For he was deceived by boys who when killing lice said to him: "What we have seen and gotten hold of, these we leave behind; while what we have not seen and gotten hold of, these we take with us."

An especially astute aphorism is the following: "Time is a child moving pebbles in a game; the ruling force is like a child."

In this aphorism, Heraclitus says the Logos forms and moves things as relative time. The Greek word nepios, used in the aphorism refers to a preverbal non-speaking child. A young child has only a basic intelligence and not a lot of knowledge. The preverbal child is a symbol for that which moves relative forms as time and nonverbal force. The pebbles were used by the child in arithmetic counting or as a game of arranging shapes or patterns, and then the pebbles were either kept for a time, or soon after discarded randomly. Like a preverbal child, the ruling force of existence that moves all as change and time, has a basic rudimentary natural intelligence displayed as order.

The ruling force does not have actual knowledge of what it is doing, it just moves all things as a play. It moves and arranges through mere chance, as a bare minimum of knowing present in inanimate and animate functions. After the counting game is over, the child eventually discards the make-shift pieces. So does the cosmic Logos scatter and discard, through disintegration and death, the numberless non-living and living forms it brings into existence.

"Good and evil are the same."

There is one cosmic force that moves each living form. Life forms having nerve endings, and all experience the same duality of the pleasures of balance and good, and the pains of evil deprivation and excesses. In this way of seeing, good and evil acts are dependently moved by the single shared Logos of existence.

"Only the one is wise; it can and cannot be called Zeus."

Heraclitus considers the Logos to be wise in some way, perhaps referring to order in the environment. The Logos can be known by the name and personality of the Greek god, Zeus. This is so, as the local sculpted figure of Zeus aids in making, what is in reality an omnipresent and nonlocal originating force, more apparent to human comprehension. However, the Logos as a cosmic force, cannot be known as Zeus. The name, personality, stories and images of Zeus, as well as other gods of the world help humans to comprehend something of the origin of things. The gods are anthropomorphic substitutes for comprehending the transcendental surround cosmic force, also immanent in the relative forms of existence.

Panta Rhei

For Heraclitus, the Logos is an unseen cosmic force, the presence of which can be observed and comprehended through three relative attributes. The first of these attributes is known by the Greek term, panta rhei, which means, continual change. In the following aphorisms, there is evidence of panta rhei as it occurs in the formations of the environment and humans.

"Into the same river you cannot step twice, for water is ever flowing."

"Cold changes to heat, and from heat to cold; what is wet dries, and what is dry becomes wet."

"The Logos is day and night, winter and summer, war and peace, abundance and lack, it changes."

These aphorisms are vivid images of reality experience as ever changing events. Heraclitus points out that the environment consisting of temperature, rain, and dryness is ever-changing. Just as water flows in a stream or river, so do moments of time as changing cycles of day and night, and season to season. The Logos is the originating cosmic force that continually transforms the relative forms of the environment and living forms. The changing conditions of war and peace, and satiety and want, are also relative processes of the Logos.

Neikos

The second attribute of the Logos is the Greek word neikos, usually translated as meaning war, with connotations of conflict, strife, struggle, and opposition.

"War is the father and ruler of all; and from it have come gods, and humans, some as slaves and some free."

"It must be known that war is universal and strife right, and that through strife all things come to be and are useful."

The Logos, like a father, brings forth relative formations in time and rules them. The originating cosmic force has brought forth the gods, which can be understood to be anthropomorphized environmental forms; for example, the ocean as Poseidon, and the storm clouds and lightning bolts as sent by the sky god Zeus. The awesome presence of these environmental forms oppose the feeble abilities of humans. Humans, in turn, oppose each other, and in so doing some become free and others slaves.

Humans oppose each other in personal relationships, sports, the economics of work and business, politics, law, and militarily. Heraclitus admonishes that it is to be comprehended that war or conflict is the universal condition of existence shared by all, and the strife that results from this opposition of forms is a law that is right and just.

Charles Darwin's (1809-1882) theory of Natural Selection, confirms the competition and strife occurring in living organisms, as individual members of a species compete for food, shelter, and reproduction. The individuals who successfully survive this competitive strife, live on to perpetuate the species, and those who are not successful die. From basic life forms of viruses and bacteria, to the largest blue whale, aggression is necessary to consume other living forms as food and to continue to exist. This said, Heraclitus found fault with the poet Homer who is said to have remarked:

"Oh that strife was removed from the lives of gods and men. For then there would be no harmony without high and low notes, or life without male and female, which are in opposition."

Reality consists of opposition, and if this were eliminated, existence would come to an end; there would be no music or reproduction. Since all things come from the Logos and struggle through existence, all is equally beautiful and good. But humans lack this perception, and instead conceive judgments of right and wrong or good and evil.

"To the Logos all things are beautiful and good, though humans suppose that some are right and others wrong."

From the cosmic Logos comes one immanent force equally present in the opposites of life and death, male and female, large and small, good and evil, and aggression and love. Humans prefer experiences that are right and good, and seek to avoid others as wrong and evil. From the point of view of the Logos which these opposites equally come from, all of them are beautiful, right and good.
Not only are humans at war with the environment, other species, and fellow humans, but they are also constantly struggling within themselves.

Each individual psyche or soul has to contend with primal willful desires.

"It is difficult to struggle with desire. It gets what it wants at the cost of the psyche."

Metron

While opposition brings about conflict and strife, it also brings harmony. The view that harmony also arises from opposing differences leads to the third attribute of the Logos, which is the Greek word metron, meaning measure or balance.

"What differs is joined, and from differences come to be the fairest harmony, and all things occur through strife."

"The kosmos shared by all, neither the gods nor humans have made, but it always was, is, and will be an ever-living fire, kindled in measure, and in measure extinguished."

Heraclitus states that the universe has not been made by a god personality, but rather it comes into and goes out of existence through metron, the immanent relative force of the Logos through limiting change. Fire is a symbol of this process. Metron is the attribute of the Logos which gives balance, and regulates the extremes of change and opposition that occur in the origin and development of varying opposing forms. For example, life forms that have come into existence through the regular measures of the environment include the solid support of elements of the earth, temperature and light from the sun, water, and air. Life comes into and goes out of existence through the metron of these opposing, yet complimentary and interdependent processes.

"They do not see how that which differs is joined. It is a harmony of oppositions, as is the bow and the lyre."

The Logos consists of opposing harmony. The parts that differ and oppose each other contribute to the overall useful function of a whole cosmos, as exemplified by the string and wood of a bow.

The bow brings death, while the strings, sound box, and neck of a lyre which, when joined, enhance aesthetic experience of music. So Heraclitus says:

"The unseen harmony is better than the visible."

It is best to see unitary relationships rather than dwell on apparent differences. Despite differences there is a depth of shared unity of apparent surface opposites.

"The way up and the way down are one."

It depends on one's perspective and location. A valley and mountaintop are connected by the same land, path, or road.

"Beginning and end are common."

A pencil tip placed on a piece of paper, and from a point slowly moved around to complete a circle, end and join at the beginning. So both are common or shared. Metron or balance is also important as it concerns human conduct on the earth.

"Self-discipline is the highest virtue, and wisdom consists of speaking truth and living in accord with physis [nature]."

The individual must discipline himself in life to acquire wisdom and to speak the truth. While differing from the inanimate environment, life is an animate unity with it.

The Logos has three attributes of panta rhei or change, neikos or conflict and opposition, and metron, or measure, balance, and unity. From one cosmic force comes the many changing and opposing forms which function as a unity of relative measure and balance. However, humankind is asleep and does not perceive these three attributes to be a function of the Logos.

"To those awake, there is one reality all share, but to those asleep, each withdraws into a private reality."

Humans fall asleep through attention to only their own ego of private thoughts and knowledge, and ignore the wisdom present in the function of relative force within all things. The Logos is a reality immediately present to the senses that consists of the effects of change, opposition, and measured balance and unity of environmental and living forms. Most ignore these attributes. Instead, humans anthropomorphize the origin of existence by attributing a human-like personality to it, and through this become separate from it. Heraclitus says:

"Although intimately joined with the Logos, humans set themselves apart from it."

Humans set themselves apart from the Logos through anthropomorphism, and the view of human-like gods who cause events. Humans also set themselves apart from the Logos by ignoring, through a lack of ability, to observe and comprehend its three attributes. Humans ignore the panta rhei or continual change, of how no two seconds are ever the same. Humans ignore how neikos, or opposition contributes to both struggle and aggression, and harmony, such as in the function of environment and life forms. Humans ignore the metron, or balance of all things, of day and night, heat and cold.

To study the laconic words of Heraclitus, one can sense the illumination of his keen observations and intuitive perceptions. His insightful words are uplifting and induce a numinous feeling of oneness with the cosmic Logos. This is especially so while looking up at a nearly full moon shining brightly in the night sky, garlanded by an infinite sea of stars.

## Chapter 11

*If one were never to see fools one could be happy for a long time,
Whoever walks in the company of fools suffers a long way,
For the company of fools as with an enemy is always painful.*
Dhammapada

*A flower wilts and falls even though we love it, and a weed grows even though we do not love it.*
Zen Saying

### Buddha

The collection of writings purported to be authentic words of the man known to history as Buddha, have been shown by scholars to contain some original sayings. The oral sayings were eventually written down and these show evidence of elaboration and editing during his lifetime or by followers during later years.

The individual who would become known as Buddha was born Siddhartha Gautama (circa 560 BCE) in North India, in what is today the small town of Lumbini, Nepal. Tradition has it that his father was a raja, a ruler of a clan of people known as the Sakyas. Siddhartha was raised a prince, eventually married, had a son, and lived a life of princely ease. However, legend says that at about twenty-nine years of age, Siddhartha realized that every human, including himself, would become ill, age, and die.

He left his family to engage in yoga and ascetic practices in an effort to comprehend the reality of life. He struggled to reach awakening through fasting, breathing (pranayama) exercises, and deprivation with little success. Finally, after six years of effort at age thirty-five, he experienced the comprehension he so determinedly sought.

In the writings of the Majjhima Nikaya, Sutta 36 are what may well be some of the actual words of Buddha speaking to an individual by the name of Saccaka Aggivessana.

"Aggivessana, then I thought, I remember once when my father the Sakyan was working in the fields. I was sitting under the cool shade of the Jambu (rose apple) tree. Separate from objects which stir desire; not harming [behaviors and thoughts] and separate from objects that harm. I experienced the consciousness of happiness and rapture, along with reflective musing, which is the first stage of meditation (dhyana) and continued in this for a time. Could this perhaps be the way to enlightenment? Out of this memory Aggivessana, came the knowledge that this is the way to enlightenment. I thought then, why should I seek to avoid this happiness and rapture which has nothing to do with objects that stir desire and nothing to do with harming or objects that harm? Aggivessana, I then thought, I will no longer seek to avoid the happiness and rapture which has nothing to do with objects that stir desire and nothing to do with harming or with objects that harm." (Majjhima Nikaya, Sutta 36)

This brief account, according to some scholars, may be some of the words of the awakened Buddha. The words also consist of a kernel and essence of his later teaching. Siddhartha Gautama's awakening came after much effort to comprehend life and death combined with a childhood memory of sitting under a cool shade tree during a family activity. He realized that objects that stir desire, behaviors, and thoughts of harming, and objects that threaten or harm are not conducive to the experience of happiness and rapture. In turn, happiness and rapture were conducive to reflective meditative musing which continued for some time. Realizing happiness and rapture and reflective musing were the way to enlightenment, he continued to increase and to further enhance these qualities of body-mind experience.

With attention not imagining or remembering pleasurable objects, or directed to harming oneself or wanting to harm others, or fearful of harm from others, one can focus more clearly on both internal and external reality. The individual can further focus to meditate for a time, to radiate and spread happiness, love, peace, and rapture successively among and through parts of the body. The experience of happiness and rapture was most probably increased through a focus of sequential visualized attention to and/or attention to feeling of individual body parts.

With the parts of the body safe and at ease, one could then reflectively muse. With a focus of attention and intention, the reality experience of radiating and spreading happiness and rapture within and among parts of the body was achieved. Also there was an increasing focus of concentration and lessening of willing and knowing.

For as long as life lasts, it is a struggle, a never-ending struggle among parts of the body, emotions, thoughts, a struggle with the environment, other species, and a struggle with fellow humans. The newly awakened one declared that when he reduced his willful struggle to obtain objects that stirred his desire, did not willfully harm himself or willfully harm others, and when he was separate from objects that could harm him, he obtained happiness and rapture of awakening. Siddhartha woke up, he became Buddha, awake!

The early account of the enlightenment experience contains within it the essence of later teachings. Meditation on the body consisting of parts probably became a practice by the Buddha in his lifetime, and later was arranged by his followers into the more formal doctrine of the Four Aryan Truths of dukkha. It is most probable that the original insight of dukkha was that happiness was dependent upon interdependent physical and mental parts. The insight (looking within) was to look at human experience in terms of functional interrelated parts, and the importance of experiencing happiness and rapture among the parts.

It is most likely that through the radiating and spreading of happiness and rapture among the parts of the body is how the dukkha teaching originated. It is more than unfortunate that the primary older teaching and emphasis of dukkha as happiness and rapture of parts became eclipsed by the prominent formula version of dukkha as suffering. Of course the other realistic side of not having happiness and rapture among the parts is to experience discomfort, struggle, and suffering. The importance of happiness and rapture of a harmony of parts became formalized later as the Middle Way or Eightfold Path.

The *Dhammapada* is a collection of sayings passed down by tradition as originally spoken by the Buddha.

The following two verses are also accepted through tradition as having been uttered at the time of his awakening:

Verse 153: Through many lives I wandered, seeking but not finding the builder of this house; ill it is to be born again and again.
Verse 154: House-builder, you are seen, no house shall you build again! Rafters and ridge-pole are dismantled. My mind has reached the unconstructed; all constructing desires now seen to end.

These two *Dhammapada* verses are similar in content to the Majjhima Nikaya, Sutta 36 verse just mentioned but are analogical. The newly awakened one found the builder of his body and ego through many lifetimes as the willing desires seen, he brought to an end.

Seeing the house-builder is the seeing of the indestructible will to live, expressed as the strong willing for food, intense willing for sex, and willing of aggression. Excessive knowing of conceptual thinking, memory, and imagination can cloud and obscure the intuitive perception of this truth. The rafters and ridgepole are the ego structure and physical body built by willing and by a distortion of knowing that ignores impermanence, how forms consist of parts, and how changing parts are not an eternal soul or self.

The Pali Buddhist word used in this instance for house-builder is sankhara; the prefix san means with, and the root suffix kar, means, to make. The implication is a process of making of things. Sankhara or willing, is the anthropomorphized builder of the house. The house-builder is willing for food, willing for sex that results in a family and the building of a house shelter, toil and care, and the willing of aggression to defend the house of life. When these are abolished, then the house builder no longer builds. Without the main support of ridgepole and the roof rafters covering, the construction ceases to exist.

How things became ill-fit-together or dukkha is sankhara, meaning willing or something will-like that moves formations into existence. Humans are connected to what moves the cosmos as the will to exist and to do. A cosmic force imparts (to grant a share) the individual will to exist.

Humans are connected directly to a cosmological force and do not need god stories, but only to clearly observe. That which moves the cosmos ever now moves within as willing for food, willing for sex, and willing of aggression. Each individual has to glimpse, observe, and quiet both willing and knowing to perceive this convincingly for oneself. This is Buddha's enlightenment.

Buddhist meditation practice is to radiate happiness, bliss, peace, and rapture among parts internal and parts external. All is moved by one "house builder," one sankhara process, one force moves all as the will to have or to harm, to pull to or push away. There is one cosmic sankhara or willing force in many forms, one not human-like house builder of all, one inner essence that moves and builds inside all forms.

Siddhartha Gautama woke up. He became Buddha, and taught until about eighty years of age when he finally died and was cremated. Relics of the great man exist, such as those found in north India in a stupa or burial mound excavated in an archeological context near the town of Piprahwa. Two finds occurred, the first during an excavation in 1898 and during a second excavation by a professional archeologist in 1971. On both occasions, burned pieces of human bone were found along with soapstone vases, and offerings of a crystal bowl with a handle in the shape of a fish. There were approximately sixteen hundred small ornaments of human and bird shapes, beads of gold and semiprecious stones. Also found were stars and flowers made of silver, gold, and pearls. The exquisite beauty of the crafted objects is convincing evidence of the high esteem held for the man who became Buddha, awake.

Three Marks of Existence

In the Hindu-Buddhist view, life is a situation of not seeing correctly, of avidya or avijja, meaning, ignorance. One is said to be a puthujjana, meaning an ordinary person but also connotes one who is considered to be cognitively impaired or deranged. Buddhists traditionally withdrew from worldly life as it was realized that existence was a madhouse of not seeing correctly.

The great fault in Buddhism and Hinduism is ignorance, not seeing impermanence, the ignoring of interdependence and relationship of parts inside and outside. Average human thinking consists mainly of surface appearance, association, and words as a reality. This is a superficial orientation which does not penetrate reality in depth. The teaching of the Buddha encourages an individual to develop vipassana, variously translated as insight, intuition, or looking within.

To be Buddha or awake, one must see experience in specific ways. The answer to the problems of life is not faith, but to see how things are in reality. So just how are things in reality? Briefly, all relative formations are said to be dukkha, consists of parts. Secondly, all relative formations are anicca or impermanent, transient, changing, and becoming-other-than. Thirdly, all relative formations are said to be anatta, not an eternal soul or self. One must practice seeing how existence consists of these three reality attributes. The way of awakening to personal salvation consists of seeing for oneself these three insights.

Dukkha

The first meditative observed mark of existence is dukkha. The early primary meaning of the Pali word dukkha is suggested in the statement of Siddhartha Gautama during his awakening.

The event was a childhood memory of sitting under a cool shade tree during a family activity. Siddhartha Gautama realized that reality experience consists of parts. A balance of parts both inside and outside was conducive to the experience of happiness and rapture, that in turn was conducive to reflective meditative musing, that continued for some time to reach an awakening experience. There is emphasis on developing the ability for meditative observation so that discomfort is reduced and balance can be reached. The bliss of happiness and rapture can then be experienced. Other words attributed to the Buddha support this view, as he spoke of four kinds of happiness or bliss to be enjoyed by a householder, by those who have not renounced the world to become a monk. These are; "The bliss of ownership, the bliss of wealth, the bliss of debtlessness, the bliss of blamelessness." (Anana Sutta)

Existence consists of internal and external parts that when balanced result in the awakening of happiness and rapture. On the other hand, if the individual is continually willing and desiring to have objects, harms self internally or others externally, or is near harmful objects or individuals, then suffering occurs. One has to live balanced so that suffering is reduced and does not increase to disorienting levels.

Of course the other meaning of dukkha is that accepted by tradition, not only by Buddhists but also by scholars. When parts are not in balance, when there is not enough or too much, suffering surely occurs. The primary insight, is that life requires balance to experience happiness and rapture. Through later tradition a secondary view developed that life is suffering.

The later and most often quoted meaning of dukkha can be observed in what is said to be an early teaching of the Buddha after enlightenment. The mentioned work shows evidence of being formalized and redacted over time. Dukkha is emphasized not as internal and external parts that require balance but as physical and mental/emotional suffering.

"The Noble Truth of dukkha is this: Birth is suffering; aging is suffering; sickness is suffering; death is suffering, sorrow and lamentation, pain, grief and despair are suffering; association with the unpleasant is suffering; dissociation from the pleasant is suffering, in brief, the five aggregates of attachment are suffering." (Samyutta Nikaya 56)

Of course coming down a narrow birth canal cannot be a pleasant experience. Neither is the process of ageing, nor is bodily illness or the process of dying. The other areas of suffering referred to include: mental/emotional experience of life, which include sorrow and lamentation, (sorrow, meaning a deep distress over the loss of something loved, while lament means a crying out loud in grief). Pain refers to acute mental or emotional distress, while grief and despair refer to disappointment and depression over loss. To be in the presence of what is not pleasant or that which is disliked is suffering, or to be separate from and not to have what is pleasant and what one likes.

Experiences of pleasure and pain occur through the five aggregates or skandhas; the relative parts or functions of the individual that are the body, sensations, feelings, willing, and the mental formations of perceptions and conceptions. The five skandhas, or relative formations of the individual consist of parts that are unstable, and so are ill-fit-together.

The basic meaning of dukkha emphasizes the fit or fitting of parts, and so the word dukkha literally means, ill-fit, an ill-fitting. Relative existence is an ill-fit; it does not fit-together well. It has a coming into existence, an ageing, and a going out of existence. While usually stable, a compound existence of parts easily becomes unstable through changes within and without. Life is an ill-fit or a bad fit. It is not a good fit but rather a bad fit, as it is made up of interdependent parts which fluctuate and eventually change, deteriorate, and degrade with time.

In an informal survey of non-Buddhists, there is a general consensus that the percentages of pleasure and suffering of life are about 50-50. For humans, suffering comes about when there is contact with some condition that is lacking, or when there is too much of some condition. Living forms suffer when there is not enough or too much. Life experience is a precarious balance which is only temporarily in a condition of equilibrium.

Living forms are prone to, and suffer, when there is not enough or too much of time, companionship, money, or possessions. Living forms consist of parts which are interdependent with other living forms, and with the environment. So there may not be enough, or there may be too much. Not having enough desired parts or having too many parts that are not desired, results in physical and mental discomfort and pain of suffering. However, a balance can be developed so that the bliss of nirvana can be experienced.

Anicca

The second of the meditative observations or insights is anicca, meaning, impermanence, transience, changing, becoming other than. All environmental and cellular formations have a coming into existence, ageing, and going out of existence.

The coming into existence occurs through the evolution of parts. These parts are transient, becoming other than, changing, having a beginning, ageing, and ending. All living forms have a conception, birth, development, ageing, and death.

A favored Buddhist way of training attention to observe impermanence is a focus of meditation on the ever changing cycle of breathing. Satipattana or insight meditation on breathing, is to clearly see; the beginning of a breath, ageing of the breath, the ending of the breath, and if a breath is short or long.

The life of a person who lives to be 75 years of age consists of 27,375 days, 657,000 hours, 39,420,000 minutes, and 2,365,200,000 seconds, each of which are unique and ever changing. No two moments are ever identical. Most individuals are stuck in time of past memory and imagined future. The only true reality is the moment of now.

Anatta

The third meditative observation of existence is anatta, meaning, not an eternal soul. The Sanskrit word atma is translated into English to mean soul. Based on the Buddha's views, the five skandhas are what the phenomenal human is, and since these parts as nouns are dukkha, (ill-fit-together and dependently conditioned,) and since these parts as verbs are anicca, (continually changing) then these formations are not an eternal soul.

Physical Body (rupa)
Feeling (vedana) physical and mental feelings of pain, pleasure, neutral
Sensation (vinnana) visual, auditory, olfactory, gustatory, tactile, mental
Willing (sankhara) acts of brain and behavior
Thought (sanna) perception and conception of reasoning, memory and imagination

To illustrate, the following words are passed down and said to be the second discourse of the Buddha to his five followers after his awakening.

The verse does not explicitly say that there is not an eternal soul but only that the body, feeling, sensations, thought, and willing are not the eternal soul.

"At Benares, in the deer park was the occasion. At that time the Awakened One said to the group of five brethren: 'Body, brethren, is not the soul. If body, brethren, were the soul, then body would not be involved in sickness, and one could say of body: "Thus let my body be. Thus let my body not be." But, brethren, inasmuch as body is not the soul, that is why body is involved in sickness, and one cannot say of body: thus let my body be; thus let my body not be.... Feeling is not the soul... Likewise thinking, willing and sensations are not the soul... Now what think you, brethren, Is body permanent or impermanent? Impermanent, lord. And what is impermanent, is that good or ill? Ill, lord. Then what is impermanent, woeful, unstable by nature, is it fitting to regard it thus: this is mine; I am this; this is the soul of me? Surely not, lord." (Kindred Sayings, Vol. 3, No. 69)

Buddha and his followers observed the problem of human life to be both a psychological ego and an eternal ego of a soul. Humans construct an ego within and also construct a superego god outside of themselves. Within changing conditioned processes of the skandhas, the body, sensations, feelings, willing and thinking, the stable entity of an ego is constructed. This activity is related to anthropomorphism, which is the conceiving and constructing of a super ego having the human-like features of a god externally. Humans egocentrically glorify their ego and their soul, and think only a greater ego of a god can save their often poorly functioning ego during life and soul after physical death.

In reality, an individual is saved or continues according to the universal law of cause and effect and personal willing, not the intervention of a super ego of a god. Humans construct a permanent ego and soul inside, and also construct a greater ego of a god outside to explain their origin. While both are a survival strategy, both are cognitive distortions, and failures to accurately observe and apperceive.

The individual must reduce and surrender ego construction both inside and outside.

Ignorance contributes to the conceived and mentally constructed ego and soul to continue to exist in unseen afterlife realms. This process is based on the law of karma or cause and effect, to be reborn again and again.

Human relationships are vulnerable to personal clashes and even more so are egoistic relationships. As Buddha commented, "Having seen the glittering golden bracelets well-crafted by the goldsmith clashing against each other on the forearm, let one live solitary like the one-horned rhinoceros." (Sutta Nipata)

Egoism is a cognitive problem both in life and the afterlife. There are a number of disciplines that seek to reduce and dismantle the obstructing ego, and to remove the barrier of separation between an individual and others. Some methods are more effective than others. Those that are ineffective include: the Middle East religion of Judaism and the early scapegoat ritual and modern Day of Atonement, the religion of Christianity and doctrine of Vicarious Atonement, and Islam in which Muslims seek to do more good than evil deeds, and through daily ritual to submit their individual will to the greater will of Allah.

There are effective ways that seek to dismantle the ego, and remove the barrier of separation between one self and others. These include: the Hindu practice of yoga and meditative calming of the body and mind, relying on and utilizing the law of cause and effect or karma, Taoism and the harmony of yin yang and chi or energy, and of course Buddhist practice of meditation and insight into dukkha, anicca, and anatta.

Enlightenment Factors

Buddha spoke on the knowing of, developing, improving, and perfecting of the Seven Enlightenment Factors. The seven factors (a factor is that which contributes to a particular result) of practice leading to enlightenment or awakening are:

Mindfulness (sati)
Investigation of the teaching (dhammavicaya)
Energy (viriya)

Rapture and bliss (piti)
Calm, relaxation of body and mind (passaddhi)
Concentration (samadhi)
Even-mindedness (upekkha)

The individual must know about each of the enlightenment factors, must develop it, must find ways to improve the enlightenment factor, and finally must find ways to perfect the enlightenment factor. Meditation and letting go of worldly interests are conditions that facilitate development of each enlightenment factor. Investigated, developed and repeatedly practiced, the seven enlightenment factors lead to clear vision and deliverance of nirvana.

The seven factors of enlightenment lead to removal of ignorance, the great fault in Buddhism, comparable to sin in Western religion. In everyday experience the mind is conditioned to remember the past and to imagine the future, as personal survival depends on these time constructs. Who would an individual be without memories, and how could he survive without anticipating and planning the future? However, this conditioning gets out of control, and individuals get stuck in the past or live a life of imagining a future that never arrives. This is not real living. Meditation practice keeps attention focused. The constructs of past and future time fall away. Meditation is training to be in the pre-sent now.

Ashoka

The teaching of Buddha was spread by missionary efforts of monks through India and beyond. Buddha's teachings were also promoted by Ashoka, a Hindu ruler who (circa 304-232 BCE) ruled northern, central, and almost all of southern India from circa 270-232 BCE. The name Ashoka means, without sorrow. In the remains of his official edicts inscribed on stone columns, he is referred to as Devanampriya, meaning, the beloved of the gods, and as Priyadarsin, meaning, he who regards all amiably.

As a Hindu, Ashoka was injured in battle, his injuries were treated by Buddhist monks and nuns, and this is how he learned of Buddhist teachings.

## Tool-Maker to God Maker

After recovering from his wounds, he married his Buddhist nurse Devi. Ashoka waged war against the ruler of Kalinga during circa 265 BCE. The Kalingas were no match for Chandashok (terrible or fierce Ashoka). Ashoka's later stone edicts report 100,000 Kalingas were killed, as were 10,000 of Ashoka's soldiers. Thousands of survivors were also deported. Legend says that after the battle ended, Ashoka, seeing so much destruction and death, became sick and uttered the following words.

"What have I done? If this is a victory, what then is loss? Is this a victory or a loss? Is this just or unjust? Is it bravery or slaughter? Is it brave to kill innocent children and women? Did I do this to increase the greatness of the empire and for prosperity or to destroy the other's kingdom and wealth? One woman has lost her husband, another her father, others a child and an unborn infant... What does this litter of corpses mean? Are these signs of victory or defeat? Are the vultures, crows, and eagles messengers of death or of evil?"

Affected by the brutality of the battle for Kalinga, Ashoka converted to Buddhist teachings. He made Buddhism the official religion of India and from about 250 BCE sent missionaries to as far away as Greece, Egypt, and Rome. He also sent out missionaries, including his son, Mahindra and daughter, Sanghamitra to Ceylon, (now Sri Lanka.). He built thousands of stupas or burial monuments, viharas or monasteries for Buddhist studies, water wells and irrigation systems, and improved roads of travel.

Ashoka practiced ahimsa, meaning non-violence, became a vegetarian, and devoted himself to the Buddhist teachings of love, seeking truth, forbearance, and obedience to parents. Later, history refers to Ashoka as Samraat Chakravartin, meaning, emperor of emperors, and his was the largest country ever to dedicate its civil laws to the ethics of ahimsa, non-harming. The symbol or emblem of modern India is taken from the capital of four lions atop one of Ashoka's stone columns. Some of Ashoka's edicts recorded on stone columns are:

"Everywhere Beloved-of-the-Gods...has made provision for two types of medical treatment: medical treatment for humans and medical treatment for animals.

Wherever medical herbs suitable for humans or animals are not available, I have had them imported and grown. Wherever medical roots or fruits are not available I have had them imported and grown. Along roads I have had wells dug and trees planted for the benefit of humans and animals."

Ashoka's edicts also show how tolerant he was of other religions:

"Beloved-of-the-Gods, King Piyadasi, honors both ascetics and the householders of all religions, and he honors them with gifts and honors of various kinds. But Beloved-of-the-Gods, King Piyadasi, does not value gifts and honors as much as he values this, that there should be growth in the essence of all religions… Therefore contact is good. One should listen to and respect the teachings practiced by others. Beloved-of-the-Gods, King Piyadasi, desires that all should be learned in the beneficial teachings of other religions."

What a contrast with Semitic Middle East religions, with such a long history of godly conflict of Jews against Christians, Christians against Jews, and Muslims against Jews and Christians, and Jews and Christians against Muslims. Further it is recorded:

"Now it is conquest by Dhamma that Beloved-of-the-Gods considers to be the best conquest…This conquest has been achieved everywhere, and it gives great joy, the joy which only conquest by Dhamma can give. But even this joy is of little consequence. Beloved-of-the-Gods considers the great fruit to be experienced in the next world to be more important."

If Europe would have followed this Aryan tradition rather than the Judeo-Christian religion of the Middle East, western culture and history would have been a much different place. The religion of Christianity emphasized suffering, death, and militarism. With little education, and little tolerance, Europe entered into the Dark Ages from the fall of the Roman Empire circa 476 CE to the Renaissance circa 1400. The profound teaching of yoga and the relaxing of the body and calming the mind and the sublime meditation and cultivation of mental hygiene of Buddhism were not to be practiced.

The teachings of Buddha later entered Europe during the early 1800's and by the 1820's interest in this Eastern religion began to develop. Not until the twentieth century and the findings of Sigmund Freud did anything come even remotely close to investigation of mental health and hygiene as did Buddhist meditation and ethical teachings. Even today, in the twenty-first century, the west has no psychology that comes close to holistic Hindu-Buddhist thinking.

In conclusion, the following comment is by theoretical physicist Albert Einstein on the religion of Buddhism:

"The religion of the future will be a cosmic religion. It should transcend a personal God and avoid dogma and theology. Covering both the natural and the spiritual, it should be based on a religious sense arising from the experience of all things natural and spiritual as a meaningful unity. Buddhism answers this description. If there is any religion that could cope with modern scientific needs it would be Buddhism."

Edward Conklin

## Chapter 12

*Change alone is eternal, perpetual, immortal. Arthur Schopenhauer*

### Schopenhauer

Personal interest in the philosophy of Arthur Schopenhauer, was piqued when as an undergraduate I happened across one of his essays entitled, *The Wisdom of Life*, in the college library. Reading the seventy or so pages was an epiphany, an awakening of deeper levels of perception. While reading his words, I occasionally experienced an uplifting sense of well-being, and would have to place the book down as I could not continue reading. I would often close my eyes and sink into a meditative reverie for a time. Family background and a mild pessimistic view of the world was the basis that prepared and attracted me to the philosophy of Arthur Schopenhauer. It has been the privilege of a lifetime to read his words that excel in clarity of thought and wisdom.

Arthur Schopenhauer (1788-1860) was the son of an astute German businessman. When his father died he lived on an inheritance, which afforded him the time to think and to write about his philosophy. Schopenhauer is known for his philosophy of pessimism, the view there is more bad or evil, aggression, strife and suffering in life, than there is good, love, and happiness. His own words are:

"When I was seventeen, without any proper schooling, I was affected by the misery and wretchedness of life, as was the Buddha when in his youth he caught sight of sickness, old age, pain and death."

Schopenhauer says an optimist would tell him to look at the peaceful beauty of the earth with its sunshine, mountains, valleys, rivers, plants and animals. Schopenhauer admits these are beautiful to behold but to be them is quite different. Existence on all levels consists of struggle, strife, and suffering. He saw humankind's attempt at optimism and theism as a cognitive effort to explain away and conceal the struggle, strife and suffering of life.

He said, "The world is just a hell and in it human beings are the tortured souls on the one hand, and the devils on the other. I suppose I shall have to be told again that my philosophy is cheerless and comfortless simply because I tell the truth."

The struggle and suffering of life cannot be explained away by religion, philosophy, psychology, or science. The individual must learn to observe and to think for himself. To only read and consider what others have written is a concern with concepts and it is only through the practice of meditation that one can arrive at one's own insightful perception and intuitive comprehension. Meditation frees attention from the service of willful individual ego concerns, to focus more on intuitive comprehension and truths. He suggests that the valuable insights obtained in meditation be written down so as not to forget them. His short essay *"On Din and Noise"* laments how every kind of noise disturbs, distracts, and diverts one from meditative focus and perception.

In his writings, Schopenhauer spoke of the origin of existence as a cosmic force that he called will. The will is the metaphysical origin beyond all natural relative phenomena of forces, energies and forms. The will is also immanent as the inner function of everything, the kernel of every phenomenon. All forces and inanimate and animate forms are objective phenomena of the will. At the lowest levels, the will is a blind striving that brings forth the forces of gravity and magnetism, the energy of quantum and atomic particles and elements of inanimate forms. The will is present as the willing and biological functions of living forms.

Schopenhauer identified human existence as a twofold phenomenon of willing and knowing. Willing is primary, and is expressed as the function of the human body, especially the genital function of reproduction. Knowing is secondary, and located in the brain that forms representations of external objects. The cosmic will is known to humans only as an individual will in the biological subconscious and conscious functions of the body.

The sole attribute of the will is striving which continues forever; no attained goal can put an end to willing. Schopenhauer remarked:

"...the will, whose phenomena is life, is a striving without aim and can therefore end only by its abolishing itself, otherwise it goes on forever. Therefore this is also expressed in everything that belongs to the world...All willing springs from a want or deficiency, and hence from a suffering, and as all life is necessarily a willing, so is it also a suffering."

Schopenhauer said of society:

"History shows us the life of nations, but it narrates nothing but wars; the years of peace occur now then only as brief periods of rest, as pauses between the acts. We thus find the life of nations to be a constant struggle, and so too is the life of the individual; he always proceeds from one conflict to another. We live in constant conflict and die with sword in hand."

As a cosmic force, the will is not observable in space and time as it moves the phenomenal forces of magnetism, gravity, elements, and all quantum and atomic particles. While the cosmic force of will moves all environmental and living forms, it cannot be observed as an object. The cosmic force of will is not observable by the human brain/mind, as it is not limited by space, time, and causality.

Schopenhauer said that "Psychologists frequently regard willing as a result of knowing, whereas the entire power of cognition is a product of the will. This is a principle and basic error." The inner essence of all things is a metaphysical indestructible will, and is not that which knows and thinks but is that which moves, urges, forms, and organizes.

He further insists:

"The will in itself although already individualized, is really not yet an I or ego, but with the addition of knowledge to the will, the I or ego first arises and is therefore at first a phenomenon in the realm of knowledge. It is a centre given to knowledge by something different therefrom, namely by the will, and moreover it would be foreign to knowledge. But without knowledge there would not even be a centre for it and hence also no I or ego.

Therefore the I first arises through the union of will and knowledge, and indeed through a union of such a kind that the will dominates knowledge."

Secondary to willing, reality for humans is representation. The brain and its function that is called the mind, is evolved by the will to provide reason and motives. The world outside as an object, is a representation in a physical brain, that the innate a priori function of reason, organizes sensations into coherent space, time, and causality. The senses and representation of external objects occurring internally in the brain is limited to know only surface appearances. The "thing-in-itself," (German, ding an sich) or the transcendental reality of a cosmic force of will cannot be known, only how things appear as representations and phenomena.

Schopenhauer said of time: "Life is like a soap-bubble which we maintain and inflate for as long as possible, yet with the absolute certainty it will burst." He also stated:

"To enjoy the present moment and make this the purpose of our lives is the greatest wisdom (for it alone is that which is real, everything else being imaginary); and it is the greatest folly, for that which in the next moment no longer exists and completely vanishes like a dream has no value. Only for one moment does the word Is belong to each event of our lives, and therefore throughout endless time only the word Was. Every evening we are the poorer by one day. We should probably be driven mad at the sight of the passing of our brief span of time, if there were not in the very depths of our being a secret awareness that the inexhaustible spring of eternity belongs to us for always renewing time and life therefrom. If there is anything, then it is this which shows us the vanity and emptiness of our existence."

Schopenhauer says that there are three ways for humans to reduce individual willing and to eventually turn the will away from the world, to remove oneself from the phenomenon of what he called "palingenesis," reincarnation of individual existence. First is the way of aesthetics, or beauty in the arts.

Entering into aesthetic contemplation of creating art, or through observing natural or artistic beauty, the relentless assertion of willing is reduced. Thereby a temporary will-less aesthetic awareness is experienced, which can better comprehend the universal significance of will in individual things.

The second way of reducing willing in the world, and of eventually turning the will away and so removing the individual from a recurring palingenesis, is ethics and morals. Ethics is the study of the basis of the act of determining right or wrong, good or bad. Ethical value judgments are usually made by a god or humans. Morals result from ethical judgments, and are the customs or rules of conduct by which humans live. Schopenhauer thought the basis of ethics and morals was compassion, "with feeling" for another. An individual consists of will and ideational representations, and this dynamic results in egoism of self- assertiveness and conflict with other assertive egos. Therefore there is perpetual conflict among humans. Ethical virtues such as sensitivity, kindness, honesty, and truthfulness make a saving purity. Virtues are the "better consciousness" rather than the empirical or sensory experience of struggle.

Humans are faced with willing good or evil. Without a doubt humans should will good as it lessens struggle and conflict while evil increases it. With better consciousness, one is lifted up higher leading away from lower consciousness that leads to an increase of chance, errors, and to harmful willing toward others. Willing what is better contributes to peace, and willing what is less good contributes to struggle and suffering. Life is a struggle which each person eventually loses but few want to give up the effort. Some look forward to the end when the struggle of life is over and one can find peace finally in death.

Schopenhauer says the third way of reducing willing is the practice of asceticism; "...from the same source from which all goodness, affection, virtue, and nobility of character spring, there ultimately arises also what I call denial of the will-to-live." Schopenhauer said that the denial of the will to live is the "salvation from life."

Schopenhauer said that the great and fundamental truth of existence contained in the Hindu, Buddhist, and Christian religions is that they teach a ..."need for salvation from an existence given up to suffering and death, and its attainability through the denial of the will, hence by a decided opposition to nature, is beyond all comparison the most important truth there can be."

While Schopenhauer says that the will is the cosmic origin of all existence, he also says that; "...the will, can be subdued by what is secondary, namely knowledge." For the individual, having a developed intellect and knowledge, one can then utilize the will to reduce willing. Saintliness or holiness consists in denial and surrender of willing. Schopenhauer spoke of the ascetic practices of Hindu, Buddhist, and Christian saints, such as fasting, solitude, and the enduring of hardships. What remains after accomplishing the abolition of the will is impossible to put into words. Schopenhauer says that if salvation is to be obtained in an existence like ours, the will must be turned from willing. The most direct way to salvation is through knowledge, and only rare individuals succeed in this effort. It is the narrow road of the few. For this way, interest, effort, and intelligence is required, and the dedication to meditation, self-exploration and observation.

Ascetic practice of self-denial reduces willing and so the individual as phenomenon. Practicing meditation and training to reduce willing for or against, he thought one could arrive at a relatively will-less experience. If the reports of sages and mystics of the past serve as a notice, a radical reduction of willing does bring joy and peace as a sense of well-being beyond words of description. Schopenhauer said:

"...it is self-evident, that which now produces the phenomenon of the world must also be capable of not doing this and consequently of remaining at rest... Now if the former is the phenomenon of the will-to-live, the latter will be that of the will-not to-live."

Schopenhauer stated:

"Behind our existence lies something else that becomes accessible to us only by our shaking off the world...to those in whom the will has turned and denied itself, this very real world of ours with all its suns and galaxies, is…nothing."

The indestructible part of humans is a pattern of willing, that after physical death remains active within the greater cosmic will. These patterns of willing can be removed by reducing willing over time to a quiescent state. The individual can make the effort to turn his will away from the will to live. Or one will not take up this effort and instead let suffering and death turn one's will away from the striving and struggle to exist.

Schopenhauer thought the most prevalent way of turning the will away from the world was that of the mass population. It is the way of sinners as are the majority of humans. This way is shown in Greek tragedy, when the hero meets with suffering as a result of willfulness. The Greek word hamartia means, "a judgment error or flaw," to make a mistake by the protagonist or hero. The error in judgment was often influenced by hubris, meaning pride that placed too much emphasis on individual will. Thereby the individual ignored fate or moira, (the daughters of Ananke the goddess of necessity) the will of the gods, and the laws of the polis. Through suffering, the hero gained insight and so reduced willing but did not turn away from the world of willing. The audience experienced catharsis, or a purging of the emotions of fear, pity, and sadness. But the Greeks had no philosophy to express this view of the denial of the will, so it was left to the viewer to get the message.

The individual has to relent, meaning to change one's mind about a course of action, especially if harsh, and to become more mild and amenable, to become less severe or unkind. The individual must relinquish every selfish and excessive controlling act which silently forges an unseen, yet real, causal path unerringly leading to personal downfall.

Willful pulling of one's own way, slowly and surely forges a self-pulled trigger that aims at one's own destruction. This is the meaning and message of the Greek tragedy plays, of hubris, self-centered pride, and forceful unyielding willing.

For Schopenhauer, Greek tragedy plays held up to view how chance, irrevocable mistakes, and wickedness corrupt and deprave even the innocent, and the noble best of humans. The suffering and vanity of life confront the spectator so as to move the individual to temporarily turn away from the egocentric willing of life. For the vast majority of individuals, the way to salvation is a slow process of trial and error learning. It is a way of gradual adjustment, as when getting into a shower or bath. First the water is too hot and then maybe too cold, so it takes some time of adjustment. With living, the adjustment can take years and many lifetimes. Through suffering, an individual will ultimately reach the denial of the will-to-live; to finally turn from the path of error that is existence, and so attain salvation.

Schopenhauer favored the view of palingenesis (Greek palin, again, and genesis, birth). He thought the will as the metaphysical basis of existence, and the basis of the body and brain, is that which survives physical death. There is an unlimited amount of time, which like quantum energy and vast galaxies, is cyclical not linear. Whoever insists on affirming their individual willing through time, and who is not converted to reducing the individual will to live, will continue in a cycle of earthly existence. Some perhaps, more sensitive humans, choose not to will to live, and exert their will to die. But the individual only destroys the appearance of the will, the body, and does not succeed in destroying the indestructible will within. So they will continue to struggle with existence again.

Subduing the will is not easy. Traditionally, fasting is a practice used to control the will to live expressed as hunger, while celibacy controls the will to live as sex and reproduction. There have been a minority of individuals who have accomplished the feat of subduing the will. Buddha fasted and lived a celibate life after experiencing Nirvana. Jesus fasted in the desert and perhaps, according to church dogma, lived a celibate life. Probably unnamed others have accomplished the task, such as monks, hermits, and religious recluses.

Kaput

Arthur Schopenhauer died September 21, 1860. His remains are interred in the Hauptfriedhof cemetery in Frankfurt, Germany. A trip to the burial site is along a small roadway with a sign directing the visitor to a walk path. Approaching the gravesite, there is a rectangular low hedge, and there one can glimpse the gravestone, a large slab of black Belgian granite. The only inscription is the name, Arthur Schopenhauer. No dates or epitaph. Once asked by a friend where he wanted to be buried, Schopenhauer replied, "No matter where; posterity will find me."

## Chapter 13

*You say "A wise one created us," this might be true we will agree.*
*"Outside of time and space," you say?*
*Then why not say at once that you favor a mystery immense,*
*That tells us of our lack of sense? Al Mar'arri*

### Metaphysical Views

The metaphysical significance of existence is mainly a question of willing. Did the environment and life come from willing? Do humans have a will, and what should the individual will on earth? Does willing continue beyond life in an afterlife? Does willing return again in a new life?

Western adopted Middle East religion says that in the beginning there was the willing of a god, and one should will the ethic of good in life and not evil. There will also will be a continuation of willing in an afterlife of either a heaven or hell. Eastern religions say, based on individual willing and karma, there will be entry into an afterlife and an eventual return to another earthly life.

In modern science, there is a great disconnect of human willing in life with the beginning, ethics, and ending of personal existence. Briefly, modern physics says that in the beginning there was no willing of a human-like god, just a Big Bang or colliding membranes of an M theory. Science says it has never found one, so humans do not have a will, and behavior is only biological and a biochemical stimulus and response to the environment. Ethically and morally humans should willingly obey social law or be punished or put to death by fellow humans. Science says that there is no evidence for a continued willing in an afterlife. For science, the individual is marooned in a brief lifetime of struggle in a seemingly endless expanse of space and time.

The human-like god of religion is one extreme, while the science of observing and measuring cause and effect change, environment, and living forms, is the other extreme.

These two pragmatic views, useful in their own way, are also roadblocks to enhanced perception and comprehension of existence.

There is a deep existential human despair produced by these two broadly developed views of theistic religion, empirical science, and theoretical physics. Each can be seen to have facets which if combined could end the delusions of both. For now, let's begin with the religion point of view and get to science along the way.

Insight or Revelation

There are essentially two main types of expression of revelation exhibited by founders of religion. After a time of seeking a better comprehension of the problem of living, including suffering and death, the answer to inner psychological conflict is resolved into one of two kinds of expressions. The sought for answer is expressed as either internal insight, or as the words of an external divine being. Looking at various religions, it is also apparent that human willing is the main problem that forms the core essence of religious teachings.

Hinduism and Buddhism obtained insights into the mystery of existence, and from the insights developed an oral and written tradition of practice. Hindu and Buddhist ascetic disciplines of yoga and meditation are ways of obtaining insight into the internal reality of body-mind functions. There is always stress among parts of the body, emotions, thoughts, and a willful struggle with others. The physical and meditative practice of yoga reduces the internal stress of thoughts, emotions, and body muscle groups, and reduces external struggle with others.

Early Hindu ascetic practices included meditation and yoga. Other practices include eating of one meal a day, fasting, celibacy, forest seclusion, voluntary enduring of pain, overcoming of fear of wild animals, abstinence from intoxicants, and renunciation of worldly possessions. Some also practiced not lying down during sleep, staying awake for extended lengths of time, all as attempts to reduce and nullify individual willing.

As did Hindus, so early Buddhists also practiced these ascetic disciplines and later codified them into writing.

Buddha taught the path of the Middle Way of willing as discussed in the teaching of the Eightfold Path. Buddhists identified the moving force of individual existence as sankhara, acts of willing that originate from ignorance.

For an individual, seeking insight and reducing internal willing and knowing, and finding an answer to how the environment and life came into existence. is difficult. It is much easier by far to project a greater human-like will and to have others accept this view. The theistic religions of Judaism, Christianity, and Islam, did not develop methods to acquire insight, instead they traveled the path of revelation, the hallucinatory receiving of words and instructions from a human-like god.

The Middle East theistic tradition can be traced to the patriarchs Abraham, Moses, and the prophets Jesus, and Muhammad. There is no method of developing discernment in these religions, only god inspired commandments demanding obedience, and communicated to others through story format. The optimistic view of these theistic religions is that a human-like god is in charge and that through punishment and reward, life will work out best for humans. The first chapter of Genesis states that all was "good" and the second chapter says oops, not all is good, there is also evil. The optimism of the first chapter of Genesis gives way to the deeper level of comprehension in the second chapter Garden of Eden story. The second chapter portrays that it is impossible to have a paradise or existence without evil being present in the environment, and humans as the evil or excessive force of willful aggression.

The Jewish god's first attempt to regulate human willing was merely a warning not to ingest the fruit from the Tree of Knowledge of Good and Evil, as to do so would bring death. This device absolved the god of bringing death into the world, which was shifted to, and became the fault of, humans.

The first humans having been created with the ability to become willful soon did so after ingesting a special knowledge laden fruit. The god then sought to regulate human willing behavior by cursing and banishing the first humans.

This strategy was not successful, as Adam and Eve then willfully reproduced, and Cain soon willfully killed his brother Abel. There was another ineffectual attempt to curb the continual evil willing of humans, "And God saw that the wickedness of man was great in the earth, and that every imagination of the thoughts of his heart was only evil continually." (Genesis 6:5) The god willfully destroyed earthly life with a flood, except for the life on Noah's Ark. Yet this disaster only mildly curbed and did not make a long term difference in human willing.

Later in Exodus are the words, "And the Lord said unto Moses, I have seen this people, and, behold, it is a stiffnecked people." (Exodus 32: 9) The Israelites are called "stiff-necked" as they would not bow, bend, or lower their heads in respect to the god's will, to leadership, and to respect each other. So in the Jewish Torah there is yet another attempt by the god to regulate excessive evil of human willing by giving six hundred and thirteen commandment laws, comprising of 248 "thou shalt" and 365 "thou shalt not" commandments throughout Exodus, Leviticus, and Deuteronomy. For pious practicing Jews, the individual had to willingly follow the commandments of the law. Yet strictly doing so was to result in the mentality of legalism that continues today in Conservative and especially Ultra-Orthodox Judaism. When the Jews strayed from the commandments and did not heed the god given warnings of the prophets, the god willfully sent the willed aggression of Babylonian, Assyrian, Greek and Roman armies, defeats, and diseases (Numbers 16:49; 25:9) to punish Jewish willfulness. This is how Jews see history, as lessons from the will of the god Yahweh to counteract human willing. So nothing has changed with willing evil on the earth and nothing ever will.

In the biblical godly jungle of legalistic commandments, can be found only a very few words to turn humans away from willing of aggression and struggle, toward the willing of love. "Hear, O Israel: The Lord our God is one Lord: And thou shalt love the Lord thy God with all thine heart, and with all thy soul, and with all thy might." (Deuteronomy 6:4-5) "Thou shalt not avenge, nor bear any grudge against the children of thy people, but thou shalt love thy neighbour as thyself: I am the Lord." (Leviticus 19:18)

It is possible to conjecture that among the many commandments, these few words of love had an influence on a northern Israelite who later founded another religion that flourished for non-Jews. Someone asked the teacher Jesus a question to which he replied:

"Master, which is the great commandment in the law? Jesus said unto him, Thou shalt love the Lord thy God with all thy heart, and with all thy soul, and with all thy mind. This is the first and great commandment. And the second is like unto it, Thou shalt love thy neighbour as thyself. On these two commandments hang all the law and the prophets." (Matthew 22:36-40)

"And, behold, a certain lawyer stood up, and tempted him, saying, Master, what shall I do to inherit eternal life? He said unto him, What is written in the law? how readest thou? And he answering said, Thou shalt love the Lord thy God with all thy heart, and with all thy soul, and with all thy strength, and with all thy mind; and thy neighbour as thyself. And he said unto him, Thou hast answered right: this do, and thou shalt live. (Luke 10:25-28)

For Jesus, the answer to reducing conflict and improving human willing was the commandment law of love, the love of one's neighbor and the love of a human-like father god. One has to use one's will to love one's neighbor, and to love the simplistic symbol of a primal parent as a father figure. Early Christians had no need for a god sculpture in stone, or a distant god far beyond human life whose access was mediated by priests. There was a need for a more human-like god. If the distant god did not want to appear on earth, then a god was needed who would impregnate a human woman, and she could bear the god's son who would then suffer like humans did on the earth. He could also remedy the human condition. Suffering humans of the time and today as well, readily identify with the suffering son of a god. An added benefit of the suffering son of a god was to serve as a vicarious scapegoat for original human sin, assure salvation in the afterlife of heaven and avoid the punishment of a hell.

Christian myth scandalizes the human-like god by having him approach a human woman in an act of intimate reproduction that mimics sexual intimacy.

If a male god impregnates a human female, this is also an acceptance and way of approving the sexual act of reproduction. Though the act resulted in the struggle of birth and life and the irreversible journey to death. Adoring the birth of Jesus at Christmastime is a way of valorizing sexual reproduction and the consequences of it in the human condition.

Jesus as the son of a god serves as a connecting link to the god. As the son of a human female, he shared human blood, was born, suffered and died as do humans. Having a god share human form is a way of forging a divine-human link. This link is only accepted to be in a single human born person of Jesus, yet by this seeks to valorize and redeem the entire human species. Jesus having a special god-like status, and having a human mother, human life is vicariously made special. Christians annually, during Christmas, celebrate the birth of the son of a parent-like god. The birth of Jesus celebration is the public link with a cosmic origin, portrayed as between the human-like god and the god-like human son. To not celebrate is considered a failure to recognize, and to vicariously share a link with the origin of existence, symbolically portrayed as a god.

The Christian mythic expression of immanence in a single individual is in simple story form. The cosmic force immanent in all is not perceived. The best that can be expressed is that the life of half-god human born Jesus is given as an example to humans to endure the struggle and suffering of life with love. If it was the god's will to conceive and to will his own son to struggle, suffer, and die a painful death, then human parents during their lifetime should expect a similar, and even worse demise for themselves and their own children. The tribulation of Jesus suggests that it is better to die to this life than to inflict suffering on others. Since Jesus was the only son of the human-like god, and since Jesus was spiritually pure and other humans are not, he provides access to the god.

Other religions do not share this direct connection with and access to the god. While Christians are separate from the god, they are vicariously connected via Jesus. For those of other religions to deny that Jesus is the son of a human-like god, is to deny the vicarious yet intimate connecting link of humans with the god.

For Jews, humans are separate from the human-like god, The sole connecting link with the god is in remembrance of when the prophets communicated with the god, and the present daily observance of commandment laws that were given; once upon a time. Today, some of the laws such as animal sacrifice and sprinkling blood on the altar are no longer followed. Other laws such as kosher food laws continue to be followed, and prayers are directed to the distant god. For Muslims, humans are separate from the god and the sole connecting link is in submitting and surrendering their human will five times daily to the greater will of the human-like god.

The true Christian message is to turn the individual will away from the world. However, the later Christian way of doing this was not by comprehending the presence of a cosmic force within, but by directing attention outside to a human-like god. Jesus spoke of a human-like god as a father and asked that the god's "will be done." The request of prayer given by Jesus says, "Thy kingdom come, Thy will be done in earth, as it is in heaven." (Matthew 6:10) Of course it is easy to see daily how the god has not at all responded to humankind on earth. Later Christian writings speak of how the god will eventually struggle with evil, wreak revenge during Armageddon, and will create an end-times lake of fire. Revelation 20:15 says, "And whosoever was not found written in the book of life was cast into the lake of fire." But even a god's willful creation of lake of fire is not enough to dissuade humans from the daily willing of evil, and to affect the non-destructible will expressed in every human.

The religion of Islam recognized the problem of human willing, and teaches that the individual must submit or surrender his or her will to the greater will of the god Allah. This theistic view seeks to reduce conflict. However, Muslims also wage jihad, a willful struggle or war against infidels to willfully get them to submit and accept the view of one willing god. For Muslims, the greater will of Allah serves to keep guard over all individual wills. Having an all-powerful will, rewards good human willing and punishes bad willing at the future time of Resurrection.

The Eastern religions of Hinduism and Buddhism produced disciplines to acquire internal insights.

In contrast, the hallucinatory revelatory Middle Eastern religions of Judaism, Christianity, and Islam, produced the ideational symbol of an external human-like god. These are two differing ways of confronting an absurd and oftentimes tragic existence of struggle, conflict, accidents, ageing, and inevitable death.

Willing of Life

Human willing is defined as the effort of cells to exist, function, and to evolve, and is the combined effort of cells and organs as behavior. Willing is not simply a choice, but a subconscious and conscious effort and longing. For example, there is an exertion of effort to not be afraid, to stay awake, to lift a heavy weight, or to stop a sneeze. These are intentional acts of willing, not merely making choices.

There is a force in cells that exerts effort to exist and to function. On a subconscious human level, cells function as effort in the beating of the heart, breathing, and digestion. Cells also exert and long for, hungers for food and thirsts for water, or feels fear and attraction. Biologically, humans develop from the unknowing yet willing, of sperm and egg to exist and unite. This sequence of willing is traced to parents and back through the long evolution of life forms. The life sequence extends to the environment, elements of energy, to forces of gravity and magnetism, and beyond these measurable forms and functions to an unmeasurable cosmic force. There is a direct connection of individual willing with cosmic force.

While cosmic force is blind and unknowing, it enters into as energy and assembles forms through cause and effect change. Humans have an evolved brain/mind to illuminate their willing process through time. On a creative level, human willing, guided by conscious awareness, mimics cosmic force by putting parts together as forms of function, such as making cars, phones, and computers.

In sleep, there is a return to an earlier expression of willing and earlier level of knowing. This earlier stage of willing is without self-awareness, and consists of willing biological autonomic functions and the earlier stage of knowing as dreams.

Many are not aware of this earlier expression of knowing in dreams which all mammals experience during REM (rapid eye movement) sleep. Most people do not remember their nightly knowing in dreams. Earlier than this stage is just willing function of cells as a biological and genetic knowing of plants and willing of bacteria and viruses, which respond only to stimuli. At the next earlier level there is blind willing energy of material forms that are without knowing. Next level is of willing energy of atoms and elements, preceded by the pure forces of magnetism and gravity. Beyond this, exists only the singular presence of a cosmic force that moves all.

Faulty Willing

Indian sages realized that personal willing was important as it was good or bad karma, a function of the law of cause and effect change. For Semitic peoples, human willing was seen as faulty or sinful, and only a human-like god had a perfect and powerful will that caused all things to exist. The first view is realistic, the second is unrealistic as there is no pure willing of good to ever be found.

The realistic good of the afterlife, usually conflated with a human-like god, is in reality the good of no longer having an earthly life. Therefore, no individual should take the struggles, conflicts, and failures of life personally. Based on an impersonal law of cause and effect, this is how existence is and must be. Individual willing can be prudent, cautious, and can reasonably delay, but cannot prevent events. Random events cannot be prevented from occurring, such as struggle, conflict, aggression, separation, illness, chance, accident, irrevocable error, ageing, and death.

Each individual thinks that if they just learn to exert their willing better or more correctly, then success and a struggle-free existence will be the result. But as each comes to find, this is not in keeping with reality.

To accept the view of a human-like god is to submit oneself to a standard of higher ethics than those of average humans. For the average individual, existence and society are at times overwhelming so there are often many chances to be unethical.

The average religious person seeks to will good and struggles with evil within and without.

The average person vaguely realizes the importance of his or her individual willing. Only a rare person is persistent and motivated enough to seek to penetrate more into the unobserved interior to glimpse conscious willing to be continuation of subconscious biological function. The average person cannot sustain an interior examination of willing and knowing. Instead most people sleepily adapt to a daily routine of culture, adopts the teachings of ritual behaviors of religion, or consults a psychologist.

The function of modern psychology is to correct faulty willing of behavior and thinking. Like religion, the practice of psychotherapy also looks at human willing that forms character and habits, and attempts to direct willing in more fulfilling directions. Freudian psychoanalysts look at faulty willing that occurred during childhood and insist that unconscious memories continue to exert unconscious effects on conscious behaviors in later life. These areas of perceptual distortion and unrealistic willing, exist as memory and habit in the subconscious, and can be removed through psychoanalysis.

God

To cognitively displace an internal process of individual willing by attributing the ability to a non-perceived and only conceived human-like external god is the basis of anthropomorphic religion. Priests and ministers early positioned themselves before the presence that underlies all relative existence and pretended to have knowledge of it.

In reality this so-called knowledge consists of theological gibberish, or foolish abstract or exaggerated attributes, such as goodness, omniscience, omnipotence, omnipresence, holiness, and in Christianity a trinity. Priests, ministers, and theologians, can only be pretenders to knowledge. They serve only as ethical guides, purveyors of what is right or wrong, good or evil based on the varied and contradictory commandments of a nonexistent anthropomorphic god.

A god is an authority figure that those in authority utilize to show that even they submit to another, just as those ruled should submit to the ruler. Authority figures bolster their rule by having the support and approval of a human-like god, and by so doing gain the support and approval of those who are ruled. Religious and governmental authorities rely on the obedience of those who are stubbornly ignorant. They rely on those who continue to hold to the view of a human-like god, a view sustained with only a tenuous wishful faith and no evidence.

For theologians, a mental idea of a god is superior and true, as compared to a mere sculpted external stone idol of a god, such as the sculptures of the Greeks, Romans, and Hindus. Yet it is an identical process whether the view of a god is built within the mind as an idea of faith, or expressed aesthetically in stone and bronze. The classical sculpted gods and goddesses never moved, and response from them was seen in various interpreted events. Eventually it was realized that the sculptures only represented ideas or concepts of human thinking, and were not real. Therefore it was not so much that the Middle East god of Judaism, Christianity, and Islam was the long awaited arrival of the true god on the scene.

It was simply that human thinking had evolved to the stage of being disillusioned with static inert stone gods and goddesses. Humans slowly moved to accept the view there had to be an unseen presence that could not be represented, and was responsible for the origin of the environment and the animation of life. Yet even the unseen god presence had to continue to be represented in thought as human-like, as is seen in the words of Paul.

"Then Paul stood in the midst of Mars' hill, and said, Ye men of Athens ...as I passed by, and beheld your devotions, I found an altar with this inscription, TO THE UNKNOWN GOD. Whom therefore ye ignorantly worship, him declare I unto you. God that made the world and all things therein, seeing that he is Lord of heaven and earth, dwelleth not in temples made with hands; Neither is worshipped with men's hands, as though he needed any thing, seeing he giveth to all life, and breath, and all things; And hath made of one blood all nations of men for to dwell on all the face of the earth.

And hath determined the times before appointed, and the bounds of their habitation; That they should seek the Lord, if haply they might feel after him, and find him, though he be not far from every one of us: For in him we live, and move, and have our being; as certain also of your own poets have said, ...we ought not to think that the Godhead is like unto gold, or silver, or stone, graven by art and man's device." (Acts 22-29)

Paul is partially correct in his view of a presence that is unknown, does not exist in a temple, does not need anything, has brought forth life and breathing and habitations of humans, and that moves all things and cannot be visually represented. Yet he sins seriously by representing a cosmic origin as human-like and therefore limited, and endowed with a thinking head.

Paul also expresses the Christian attitude toward sexuality with the following words; "Walk in the Spirit, And ye shall not fulfill the lust of the flesh. For the flesh lusteth against the Spirit, and the Spirit against the flesh: and these are contrary the one to the other...." (Galatians 5:16-17)

In these words, Paul conceives of the individual will to exist, to live, and to reproduce, the sexuality of the flesh, as opposed and contrary to a Spirit, the attitude of an asexual human-like god. By spirit, Paul was also referring to the higher spirit of what humans are capable of, as in the spirit or attitudes of love and forgiveness. However, Paul's sin is a cognitive error as he kept to the only way that he and others he spoke to could recognize, that which transcends human experience; the immature anthropomorphism of a human-like god.

Outside to Inside

Humans have from birth onward, developed the life-long habit of directing attention outside to nourishment, relationships, and to objects. To counter this life-long behavior requires the spending of some time each day with meditative attention directed inside the body and mind. Then after some time, the harmful habit of directing attention almost exclusively outside to surface appearances can be corrected.

Western countries have a long history of not meditating and not observing, the intimate exchange of air, water, and food, from outside to inside, and back again. Modern humans in the environment have become like pigs in a pigsty, eating garbage food and living in a toxic chemical waste product environment. Only recently during the 1950's has the population of the United States become aware of ecology. Most times political interests and the economy is elevated to priority over the environment.

Looking inside through meditation one can observe how external energies of environment are continually transferred and transformed into physical and psychological functions within. Most do not have time to practice meditation to observe this process, as humans are busy pursuing pleasures and surviving relationships, the economy, and a consuming culture. Meditation reduces distraction so as to better observe the continual transfer of energies from outside to inside the body. Humans toil and stay busy in life, complacent with working, reproducing, socializing, and consuming with the traditional religious view that during life, and at the time of physical death, all will be taken care of by a human-like god. Only a very small minority of humans, probably less than one percent, practice a discipline of observing phenomena inside and outside, and attempt to meditatively perceive and comprehend. Consequently, most humans have the attention span of a gnat.

The universe is in continual change and motion, it is a phenomenon of super animism. What moves all things into existence is a greater cosmic force, not a human-like god. Functions on the inside of living forms, have come from an outside cosmic force through cause and effect change. The transition from a cosmic force to relative forms is an acausal process. The process is acausal as it cannot be observed. Only what has come from a cosmic force can be detected and studied.

A causeless or groundless cosmic force outside, formed all relative environmental and living forms. From a nonvisible cosmic force of cause and effect change, came an animating impetus to construct all relative visible forms. To use an analogy, from non-visible conditions of air, moisture, and temperature, particulate raindrops and snowflakes appear as weather phenomena.

Raindrops are individual but all share H2O energies of elements. Simultaneously there exists both, differing forms, yet identical sameness of energy from which rain has come into existence.

## Maker of All

The maker of all universes and dimensions is outside but how can it be perceived? The causal maker of existence can only be perceived as activity and effects. As astronomers look through telescopes into space, they can observe the formation of vast stellar gas clouds, stars and galaxies. There is, behind this activity, there an unseen former, a maker of forms that cannot be said to be human-like. Some might say the activity of the observable universe, is the willing of a god at work, creating. But there is zero evidence for this view; the unseen former of formations is what can only be called a cosmic force. A cosmic force blindly brings things into existence, there is no intelligence or care associated with the process. Humans cannot look for comfort to the cosmic force of things, as every expression of it is in perpetual struggle and conflict, beset with eventual destruction.

The maker of all things has no intelligence, thoughts, emotions, or motives. It is an unmeasurable blind cosmic force that moves the measurable forces of magnetism and gravity, atoms and elements, environmental and living forms. The maker of all things prefers to strive and struggle forever through endless time, and in terms of direction it prefers circles. The maker does not care. Based on artifact evidence, ninety-five percent of all living species are extinct, and all twenty or so of hominid species are extinct except one; Homo sapiens sapiens or modern humans.

The Cretaceous Tertiary mass extinction that occurred some sixty-five million years ago may have been caused by an asteroid over nine miles in diameter. The impact caused, or contributed to the extinction of the dinosaurs and half of the species on earth. As recently as circa 13,000 BCE on the North American continent, an asteroid or comet impacted an area in Canada causing the Holocene Extinction Event. The asteroid or comet impacted a glacier over the continent, and so did not leave an impact crater.

Remains of small spherical magnetic grains, as well as nano-diamonds twenty thousand times smaller than the width of a human hair, show evidence of the mass extinction event. Many animals went extinct including mammoths, camels, giant beaver, saber tooth tiger, American lion and many other mega fauna.

The cosmic maker only brings forth and does not care to preserve or protect. Cosmic force is continued in the individual willing to exist and to live as the desire to eat food, the desire for sex, and the desire for aggression. These three behaviors are a relative continuation of a cosmic force.

The effort and strife of existence from non-living to living can be circuitously traced. The greater observable universe of hydrogen and helium gas clouds, stars, galaxies, planets, moons, asteroids, and comets, are all in a perpetual unknowing movement. So too is the environment of the earth, evident in plate tectonic movement of earthquakes and volcanoes, temperatures of heat and cold, flood and drought, tornados, hurricanes, thunder and lightning. All of life exists as perpetual relative change. Viruses and bacteria are the earliest life forms and continually change and adjust to conditions of the environment. Animals evolved from simple into more complex forms, and developed muscles and a mouth with which to hunt and eat other life forms.

All prehistoric and historic religions seek to point to, and to communicate about, a transcendental maker from which has come the beginning of time as forces, elements, environment, and living forms. The mental image of a human-like god conceived and developed in the mind retards and obscures the evidence of a cosmic panorama for a narcissistic and theistic story of a special creation by a human-like god. Unfortunately, the best way humans can care for each other is via the projected image of a human-like god who cares for humans. A god is a reflection of the human need to have protection in the present and future, and to know the beginning of things.

Humans project their own ability of knowing and doing to a human-like god, who did things in the past, does now, and will do in the future.

This is the blindest of faith, as there is zero evidence. Having a human-like god is a strategy to remain optimistic, and to go on living despite the stress and suffering of existence

Most could not bear life without something higher to appeal to. Having a human-like god is a tactic to civilize animalistic human behavior. To not accept the view of a human-like god is to be without protection from both the god, and the aggressive behaviors of a warring group, including other religious believers. Individual struggle brings existential angst, so the vulnerable individual turns for protection to a human-like god and to the collective group of the religion. Not having a human-like god or a religion is to struggle alone and to be fearful. Accepting there is a greater human-like god and having the collective support of a religious group, an individual can somewhat relax his vigilance in life and even enjoy passing moments in an act of religious faith, trust, and relative safety.

Humans struggle into, through and out life, and there may be struggle in an afterlife as well. During the struggle and strife of life, many people traditionally look forward to a future in a place or places of an after-life dimension. But in the story tradition of theistic religion, even the afterlife realms offer little safety and peace. Christian myth says there was, and/or will be a struggle and conflict in heaven between the god and his angels, that some theologians interpret as having happened in the past, and others see as occurring in the future end times of Armageddon.

"Now war arose in heaven, Michael and his angels fighting against the dragon. And the dragon and his angels fought back, but he was defeated, and there was no longer any place for them in heaven. And the great dragon was thrown down, that ancient serpent, who is called the devil and Satan, the deceiver of the whole world--he was thrown down to the earth, and his angels were thrown down with him." (Revelation 12:7-9)

As stated, struggle, conflict, and aggression did occur in the heaven of the past and/or will occur in the future heaven. Based on the Christian religion, not only will each individual struggle, be in conflict, and experience aggression while alive on the earth.

Struggle, conflict and harm will continue in heaven as noted above, or in an afterlife dimension of hell where some human souls will continue to struggle and experience conflict through punishment.

Hell is considered to be a place of punishment for harmful human acts of willing while upon the earth. Hell is said to be ruled by a Devil that willfully inflicts harm upon humans. This view of conflict in both heaven and in hell is mainly a metaphor for a truth based observation. With few exceptions, all of existence is in perpetual struggle and conflict both here and hereafter.

Glimpsing the vast panorama of environmental and living forms in a blind perpetual struggle and conflict, who could ever again accept the fairy tale of a good and beneficial human-like god? Just the idea of a human-like god would be like a bad taste in the mouth. The individual would want to spit it out and quickly cleanse the tongue with fresh natural spring water as soon as possible.

Theism Versus Cosmic Force

Theologians and religious leaders say of evolution that it is a lie but they speak out of ignorance and worse. They speak only to those asleep struggling to survive work, finances, and fellow humans. Those asleep tolerate such crazy statements by authority figures of religion. The average person has no time, is not interested, or is not intelligent enough to investigate the many audacious and false claims of theistic religion. Even if time is allotted to investigate, a curious individual most often reads dogmatic scriptures of Judaism, Christianity, and Islam, or theistic self-help books, all of which are dead ends to reliable knowledge and wisdom.

Rather than investigate the evidence of evolution, most humans, have in the past and continue to do so today, prefer simplistic stories of a human-like god. Yet there is no observational evidence for the stories of religion, only faith (Latin fidere, trust) as a misplaced trust. There are 14 million Jews, 1.6 billion Christians and 1.3 billion Muslims, which is almost half of the population of the earth. The numbers are no guarantee of the truth of these theistic views. They are just the greater lowest common denominator of humankind.

These theistic and optimistic views that a human-like god made the best of all possible worlds is a pragmatic yet cognitive delusion. Yet to not have the presence of a god in the past, now, and not to have one in the future, is a risky view for the average person. How else can the past, present, and future be explained to the satisfaction and comfort level of the greater number of average unlearned human beings?

Existence can be more realistically and sanely explained without a god figure. This can be accomplished by asking the question, "What is inside of environmental and living forms?" The answer has to be energy. What is the determinant of that energy, and what is present that is supporting and determining energy? Based on observation and testing and not story, it can be said that the forces of magnetism, gravity, and strong and weak nuclear forces determine energies. But what is present, and what exists to move these pure relative forces? The answer is an impersonal greater cosmic force that is not human-like at all. A greater cosmic force is aseitical, (Latin, not derived from anything else) it is without any other basis, is groundless, and is not dependent on anything; everything is a relative and dependent on it.

The presence of cosmic force as immanence and why it functions in a relative way is a mystery for now and probably will be forever. This transcendent process is not observable and therefore is not able to be verbally and conceptually explained. It cannot be said what a cosmic force is like; it isn't like anything, it has no attributes. It is sui generis, of its own kind. Therefore, we can only infer, such as with the example, "Where there is smoke there is fire." Suffice to say, a cosmic force is an activating presence that prefers to condense as circular movement of forces and energies, and for living forms as cycles of life and death. The activity of the universe is readily observed, and therefore there is some presence doing this as a greater force of relative forces, energies, and inanimate and animate forms.

The roots of all existence extend not to a human-like god but to a field or ground of cosmic force. The presence of a cosmic force can only be inferred and intuited. It is perhaps possible to comprehend and to experience oneness with this cosmic force, through assiduous meditation.

A cosmic force cannot be comprehended as a story that requires an unknowing blind faith told in primitive religious metaphors and anthropomorphisms.

## Pathological Rituals of Theistic Religion

When pondering the origin of existence, the cognitive abilities of early humans were handicapped with the use of anthropomorphism. Where things came from and the cause of things was most often a human-like god. Later evolved a wise few individuals in India and China who developed and practiced intuitive meditation. In this way they more closely observed and focused on internal mental and physical processes, and on the processes of the environment. By 700 BCE Hindu rishis developed the view of Brahman, a non-human energy presence. Circa 500 BCE, another Hindu son, Buddha, taught his highly developed view of existence that did not include a human-like god. The wise few of China developed the view of Taoism and the importance of learning, not from a human-like god, but from learning and living in harmony with the natural environment.

In contrast, theologians in Medieval Europe lacked wisdom, meditative practice, and intuitive perception. Theologians were estranged from nature, and relied more on scholastic knowledge based on the writings of Aristotle and later Thomas Aquinas. Theologians argued using logically conceived ideas, relied on simple faith to comprehend the supposed existence of a Middle East derived human-like god. The Middle East religions of Judaism, Christianity, and Islam, are primitive conceptions and justly deserve to be condemned for their barbarity. They are each blood for blood atonement religions, and to be one with the god, blood must be shed and offered.

The theistic delusional view of a human-like god in Middle East religions, over time, resulted in irrational and pathological rituals. The early scapegoat ritual, sought to remove the sins of the Jews by transferring them into a goat, then thrown off a cliff and killed as an offering to Azazel. The similar and modern kaparot (atonement) ritual is conducted in preparation for the Jewish holiday, Yom Kippur.

What is emphasized in both the ancient and modern ritual is the substitute offering of blood and life, so the blood and life of humans would be spared from the god's wrath and punishment.

The kaparot ritual can be performed anytime between the New Year holiday of Rosh Hashanah and the Day of Atonement, Yom Kippur. During this time Jews ask for forgiveness of sin and guilt for deeds against the god and fellow humans. Performed mostly by Ultra-Orthodox Jews, the kaparot ritual makes use of a live white chicken, symbolic of purity. The chicken is passed over the head of the individual three times while reciting words asking the god to not punish the individual during the coming year. It is asked of the god that the punishment instead be transferred to the chicken, a rooster for a male and a hen for a woman. Words of prayer may include, "This is my replacement, this is my substitute, this is my atonement. This chicken shall go to death and I will proceed to a good long life and peace."

Biblical verses from the book of Psalms are read praising the god for saving those in the underground pit of death known as Sheol. The chicken is then slaughtered according to kosher rules by draining the blood, and the chicken is taken home to be eaten by the person, or given to charity. In large gatherings, chickens are available for purchase. More liberal or reformed Jews may substitute a fish, or money wrapped in a white cloth which is later given to charity. The modern practice of using a fish or money omits the most important part of the ritual, the substitute shedding of blood.

Another irrational and pathological ritual practice in the religion of Judaism is circumcision, the ritual removal of a section of foreskin of the male penis. The Jews accept that the ritual practice began with a mention in Genesis 17:10-14 of circumcision as a commanded practice by the god as part of the covenant with Abraham. The practice is also mentioned in the book of Joshua 5:4-7. However, older evidence of the practice of circumcision comes from a carved and painted tomb scene in Egypt dating to circa 2340 BCE.

Egyptian circumcision is thought to have been performed by a priest, using a stone blade during a public ritual. Circumcision was also required as a practice of cleanliness, to serve in worship of the god.

Priests were also required to remove body hair by shaving and plucking, and even eyelashes and eyebrows.

A modern theory also recommends circumcision, for hygienic prevention of smegma, a waxy oily sebum exuded by the foreskin covering. However, research has found that all mammals produce smegma. Smegma provides a protective coating and a lubricant; it moisturizes and keeps the glans or head of the penis soft and smooth and also has antiviral and antibacterial properties. Human females also produce smegma around the clitoris and labia minora folds. Smegma is not unclean and performs an overall protective and lubricating function.

From Judaism to the first Christian ritual of circumcision, the practice has generated pathological thinking and behaviors. As required by Jewish tradition, an infant boy must be circumcised on the eighth day after birth. In the gospel of Luke 2:21, there is mention of the circumcision of the infant Jesus, founder of the Christian religion. "And when eight days were accomplished for the circumcising of the child, his name was called Jesus, which was so named of the angel before he was conceived in the womb."

A mention of the circumcised foreskin of Jesus was first made in the Syriac Infancy Gospel dating to the 500's CE. What later became known as the "holy prepuce or holy foreskin" relic turned up in the year 800 CE, when Charlemagne gave it as a gift to Pope Leo III. Charlemagne's story was that an angel had brought the holy foreskin of Jesus to him while he was in prayer. Nice gift!

During medieval times, as many as twenty-one churches claimed to have the original holy foreskin, and many miracles were attributed to it. Amusingly, during the 1600's, the theologian, Leo Allatius, wrote that the foreskin was no longer on earth, and that when Jesus ascended to heaven, his foreskin also ascended. In his speculative view, the foreskin may have become the rings around the planet Saturn. How completely bizarre!

The holy foreskin which was located in Calcata, Italy, was venerated for hundreds of years.

In 1900, due to controversy about the existence of other holy foreskins, the Roman Catholic Church proclaimed that anyone speaking or writing about a holy foreskin would be subject to excommunication. In the year 1954, the Vatican ruled that anyone speaking of the holy foreskin would thereafter be excommunicated and declared as "infamous and to be avoided." In addition, the official Day of the Holy Circumcision traditionally observed on January 1 was removed from the church calendar. In 1983, the holy foreskin at Calcata was either stolen or turned over to Vatican authorities. To date no holy foreskins are known to exist.

Another pathological Christian ritual is the Catholic mass, during which the human-like god transubstantiates, or changes the plain bread and shared wine, into the body and blood of Jesus. Ingesting the bread and wine transubstantiated by the god into the body and blood of his son, is a primitive and barbaric way of uniting the individual with the separate human-like god. In Jewish thought, the life is in the blood, and there was prohibition by the god against ingesting it as shown from the following quotes. "But flesh with the life of it, the blood of it, you shall not eat." (Genesis 9:4) "Only be sure that you don't eat the blood: for the blood is the life; and you shall not eat the life with the flesh." (Deuteronomy 12:23, World English Bible) The Christian doctrine of transubstantiation and practice of ingesting the blood of Jesus plainly violates Jewish law and the words of the human-like god.

In no other religion but Christianity can an individual so easily join with a distant human-like god, by ingesting bread and wine that has changed into the body and blood of the god's son. This thinking is based on the crassest superstition. The individual has the opportunity, provided only by the priest, to be hand-fed and to ingest the god's son, by an easy gustatory assent and so doing, to be one with the god.

This practice has to be the zenith of religious dishonesty, pandering, and shared pathological thinking by both church officiates and member participants. In the practice of Christianity, the early blood offering of animals was done away with in favor of the more perfect offering on the cross of the half human son of the god.

"But Christ being come an high priest of good things to come, by a greater and more perfect tabernacle, not made with hands, that is to say, not of this building; Neither by the blood of goats and calves, but by his own blood he entered in once into the holy place, having obtained eternal redemption for us." (Hebrews 9:11-12)

The Islamic view and practice of blood offering is similar to Judaism and Christianity. The Arabic word, qurban, means an offering or sacrifice to the human-like god Allah. For those who give their lives in jihad and die as martyrs, their spilled blood is an offering or qurban. At the birth of a child, there is a ritual killing of a sheep or goat as a blood offering and the reciting of such words as, "O Allah, here is the offering for my son (the name mentioned) its blood for his blood, its flesh for his flesh, its hair for his hair, and save my son from the fire."

The Eid al Adha, or festival of sacrifice, is a holiday celebrated by Muslims worldwide. It is performed to commemorate the act of obedience to Allah by Abraham, when the god told him to kill his eldest son Ishmael as an offering (zabh). Iblis (Devil) or Shaitan (Satan) attempted to convince Abraham not to be obedient to the god. Abraham submitted to the god's will and prepared to offer his son. The god intervened and provided a lamb substitute instead.

Today Muslims around the globe who can afford to do so, make a blood offering by slaughtering a sheep or goat, sometimes done in a slaughterhouse. The meat is then consumed and/or distributed to friends, or to the poor. As Muslims remember Abraham's submission to the god, the ritual also reminds them of the importance of submitting their own will to the god. Some Muslims suggest it is obedience to the god in the slaughtering of the animal that is the true offering, not the blood and body of the animal. If this offered explanation is true, then why the senseless imitation of an act that is supposed to have occurred so long ago, and the senseless death of so many innocent animals through the years?

It is the blood of the offering that is important. In the Quran, the human-like god is said to have made living things variously from water, clay, and blood. "We made every living thing from water." (Surah 21:30)

"We created the human being from mud, like the potter's clay." (Surah 15:26) Surah 96 of the Quran begins with the words, "Read in the name of your lord who created, created man from a clot of blood...." Allah made the blood of both animals and humans, and so the life blood is given back in offering to the original maker of it.

Since for Muslims, the blood of humans is more valuable, the blood of an animal is a substitute. Blood offerings of a sheep, goat, cow, or camel are also made by Muslims at the tomb of a saint to obtain their help, to insure and bless a harvest, and to insure a safe ocean voyage. Blood offerings are also made during an eclipse of the sun or moon, while making a vow or oath of commitment, and on the occasion of a new business endeavor. There are also blood offerings during the setting of a foundation of a house, in time of disease or epidemics, and to atone for a sin or wrongdoing. In the slaughter and offering of an animal, one gives to the god the life blood of the animal in place of his own. Blood is special, as the excess loss of it brings death and is therefore associated with the animating of life. Blood is also unique, as the color red is missing from most of the Middle East environment.

Another irrational and pathological function in the religion of Islam is the practice of prayer. Muslims have an obsessive schedule of prayer five times daily, more than any of the other religions. Whether of pagan or Zoroastrian origin, this daily zeal clearly reveals the slavish obsessiveness of the religion with its view of a human-like god. There is an apparent human insecurity in the need to excessively communicate five times daily with a god. One has to wonder, doesn't the god have better things to do than to listen to a plethora and burdensome deluge of human requests and confessions?

However, the view of the human-like god is necessary in the Islamic cultures, and mainly functions to maintain a stable social order. The greater god ego is the demand for the submission of all lesser human egos, and therefore the result is interpersonal order and salaam or peace.

A Muslim is one who submits to the will of the human-like god, Allah.

In reality, there occurs submission and mutual human agreement to a way of socially expressing the will to exist and live. Group prayer in the mosque with its behavioral rakahs of ritual prostration, reinforces psychological and emotional solidarity among the attendees. The high frequency requirement of ritual prayer strongly indicates the tendency for interpersonal hostility and aggression in the culture, most likely caused by a less than comfortable hot, rocky, and harsh sand desert environment, and social traditions. Having the fervent view of the greater ego of a human-like god is the psychological tactic of overcoming these disadvantages.

Stories

Yearning and longing to have an intelligent parent god to explain past, present, and future time is difficult to remove from human thinking. Utilizing evolved human intelligence and observation, this can be done. It requires the discarding of religious stories and traditions of the past, and observing the present moment.

Most humans are too sleepy to be awake in present now moments. Human attention is distracted by a focus on past and future relationships of food, family and work, by television entertainment, movies, computers, reading, and cell phones. Individuals are obsessed with consuming and ever searching for a direction to greener pastures. Some leisure time is needed to investigate and to see that all stories of human-like gods are not history but artistic imagination. The realization of this fact, can be likened to being suddenly splashed with cold water. Reaction could be one of shock and anger, or reaction could be surprise and more alertness, even stimulated and refreshed by the cool water.

Not seduced by story, one has to shake off sleep time comfort stories of a human-like god. All stories of religion are the result of imagination, and are symptoms of a failure to observe and perceive reality. The view of a god is an intrusion of imagination that reduces and distorts the effectiveness of observation and perception. A human-like god is never perceived, but was and is always, imaginatively conceived. A god furnishes a causal explanation of effects, and provides a greater authority figure to demand obedience of humans, via ethical rules of conduct and ritual.

## Maker

In the Garden of Eden story, the parent god took his own knowledge of both good and evil and placed it on a tree where humans easily accessed and ingested the fruit growing thereon. The good and evil knowing god further brought forth a deceptive serpent that easily convinced naïve humans that the god-like knowledge was good to have, and the fruit was good to eat. The mythic story expresses regret for knowledge of sex and reproduction, hunger for food, and aggression, and a poignant longing for earlier times when this knowledge did not exist. The story also express a regret for a time of oneness with a human-like god who non-sexually made humans, but also illogically designed them with genitals for sex.

Newly made by the god, the Genesis story portrays humans as having only a nascent curiosity and a knowledge potential for disobedience, and these qualities reflect how they were made by the god. Soon the flawed knowledge of the god was acquired by humans. After acquiring it, humans began to make use of that flawed knowledge. The godly knowledge utilized was of course, sex and reproduction, knowledge of jealously and envy, use of aggression by one male toward another that resulted in the death of one of them. The faulty knowledge of the maker of life, is displayed in the acquired knowledge and behaviors of humans. In reality, the flawed knowledge of the god, is the limited and flawed knowledge of the Jews as they attempt to solve the cosmological mystery and the ethical problem of a good and evil existence.

Using analogy, it only makes sense that if a brand of a car functions well over time, the maker is praised. If the product malfunctions in a harmful widespread way, the maker accepts the blame and responsibly and quickly acts to correct it. There has been no correction of human-kind, as humans endowed by their maker, act with a "free will." The god does not remedy the faults of ignorance, aggression, and murder. The maker is either impotent or does not consider it important enough to change the life quality of humans, and is limited only to punish outcomes of behavior in an afterlife.

In the distortion of monotheistic thinking, only through hellish torture in an afterlife, can the human product be made better or improved by the god. Meshuga! No sane modern person can continue to accept this theistic way of seeing the situation of humankind.

In the future, monotheistic religions will be seen as furnishing a higher protective model for humans to ascend toward from a lower dependent level of development. Yet, the monotheistic religions will be much more to blame for furnishing an egocentric distortion and detrimental delusion for the mass of humankind. Theistic religions will be more correctly proved to have been an impairment of perception and human mental health. The human-like god of theistic religions is imaginary, and is therefore a faulty way of dealing with the struggle of daily life.

Strategy

The concept of a human-like god who observes and intervenes in the lives of humans is a reflex response, perhaps originated in part from those who glanced into the vast unending distance of space and endless time. To alleviate existential angst, the human image of a greater god was conceived. A god continues to be used to delimit unknown cosmic vastness and serves as a safety barrier to reduce vulnerability and fear. Supported by a human-like god with greater intelligence, humans are safe to exist in an unknown vastness of space and time, on an unsafe earth.

The unlimited ability of a human-like god, counteracts the sensing of a limited individual existence, in an unlimited space and time. If human willing behavior is ineffectual, then the greater willing behavior of a god is imagined and mentally utilized as a tool to reinforce individual willing behavior.

A god is an insular cognitive buffer, a barrier erected by humans and retained by mutual agreement to think in this way. The caring human-like god insulates humans from the uncaring, impersonal, and harmful ravages of time, environment, accidents, disease, and death. This is what a god is for.

A supportive god is a mental maneuver to get humans through another hour, day or night, week, year, and lifetime. A human-like god is projected above and beyond to protect and guide an individual through the danger filled course of life and death experiences. An individual who is converted to this view at once feels relief from personal despair.

The average person, through the sequential experience of events, senses the fluid and flowing quality of time. So an anchor is needed, a god that explains the vast origin of existence, time, and the future of where time is flowing. A god is an acknowledged and shared idea, accepted on faith, an unknown anchor in an unlimited ocean of space and time. The majority of individuals need the company of a god that prevents them from being swept away on the cosmic currents of time into nothingness.

Middle East religions say that following death, the individual is heading to a heaven or hell, a physical resurrection of dead bodies, and a judgment. The religions of India say the individual is heading in a circle of endless time and dimensions. Therefore, not a god, but the individual, brings his own repeated existences to an end on earth, and seeks to evolve to higher levels of an afterlife reality.

In an effort to reduce the evils of human existence, theists meet in a religious group to exert their attention in the direction of something good, conceived of as a god. Getting together in ritual, is a practice of strengthening individual courage to continue to exist, to affirm the will to live, and to survive the vast unknown nothingness of past, present, and future time. Each individual joins his or her own weaker willing with the imagined stronger willing ally of a human-like god. Not to do so, the average person will lack direction and become helpless, and worse, is more likely to inflict evil or excessive force upon others. Having a god is a way of seeking some greater good among a large array of earthly evils.

Modern Physics

General science is a strategy to survive and an attempt to improve the human condition.

The view of science is that humans are limited by conditions, have come from a nonexistence and will have a future oblivion. Humans have evolved from earlier species to which he or she owes their parent origin. No living species owes their existence to a human-like god.

A letter from a child to Albert Einstein asked if scientists pray to a god, to which Einstein replied:

"Scientific research is based on the idea that everything that takes place is determined by laws of nature, and therefore this holds for the action of people. For this reason, a research scientist will hardly be inclined to believe that events could be influenced by a prayer, i.e. by a wish addressed to a Supernatural Being."

Rather than a human-like god, modern physics has developed quantum theory to better explain existence. Entanglement is a term used in quantum theory to describe the way energy particles, such as photons or electrons, having interacted with each other locally, retain an entangled connection non-locally. Once in contact, for these two objects causality is not limited by space and time. Quantum entanglement endows particles that are separated by vast distances to affect each other instantaneously, and are not limited by the speed of light.

The theory caused discomfort to physicists of the time. Albert Einstein opposed the theory, and commented on quantum entanglement as spukhafte Fernwirkung, meaning, spooky action at a distance. In the Einstein-Podolsky-Rosen thought experiment paper, Einstein argued that there are two ways to explain the entangled phenomenon. The first, he said, is that there must be hidden variables within the particles that determine the particle behavior. The second comment is that the particles do affect each other faster than light, and is what he called, spooky action at a distance. This latter possibility he did not want to accept. However, quantum entanglement was experimentally verified in 1972 and in following years.

What roughly occurs during entanglement, is that two or more quanta or particles, such as electrons or photons in local interaction, instantaneously share a single quantum state, of spin or polarization. When the property of spin of one of the entangled particles is later measured, and the other particle is no longer local, even millions of miles or light years away from the other, one of them acts in the same or the opposite direction of spin instantaneously or at the speed of light. Some physicists estimate as much as ten-thousand times the speed of light. If a measure or change is made to one, the other separate particle immediately "knows" what the other is doing.

Conceptually, at the basic level of reality there is identity of cosmic force with any and all relative energy particles. As to how a cosmic force condenses into particles, will forever remain unknown. This process is acausal, as there cannot be observation of it. The transition from cosmic force into relative particles is irrational, is not rational or has no ratio or measure. Since there is no perception, there are no concepts or ideas that can portray the process.

Quantum particles are ever connected in space and time via a cosmic force until they return to the ground from which they have come. Electrons and photons consists of the same cosmic condensed force. Local particles of electrons and photons, once entangled and then separated, behave non-locally. They behave non-locally as they share the same cosmic force, are different yet a unity, and regardless of space and time, a paradox.

John Stewart Bell (1928-1990) was a quantum physicist who developed what is known as Bell's Interconnectedness Theorem. The work has been referred to by some as the "most profound discovery of science." A blue plaque at Queen's University in Belfast, Northern Ireland, where Bell studied physics from 1945-49, refers to him as both "physicist and philosopher." His work has also been referred to as "experimental philosophy." The reason he is considered a philosopher, a lover of wisdom, is that in his work he approached the boundary edge of the origin of reality. This is what Bell called the non-local unknown determinant variables of quantum particles and events.

Bell arrived at the boundary edge of an impersonal cosmic force, an unmeasurable super-force of all relative forces and energy particles and forms. For Bell, there cannot be any knowledge of measurable variables or relative causal determinants of a cosmic force or ground, nor of entangled and interconnected particles.

Physicists continue to search, observe, and may yet solve the puzzle of quantum entanglement. Science continually revises and expands its compendium of knowledge. For example, during the 1920's, the accepted view of the universe was that it consisted of only one galaxy; the Milky Way galaxy containing the earth, other planets, sun, and uncountable stars. Edwin Hubble (1889-1953) an American astronomer changed the limited prevailing scientific view of the universe based on his observations through the Mount Wilson telescope located in California during the years 1922-23. He published his paradigm changing findings in 1925.

Many astronomers opposed Hubble's discovery and evidence of countless other galaxies. One commentator made the comment that astronomers of the time went into "existential shock" after Hubble presented convincing evidence of a multitude of other galaxies. Today, one conservative estimate is that there are over one-hundred billion galaxies. Research will continue to discover other profound phenomena. One day if the species survives, science will come to arrive at a unity with that which is not phenomenon, that of an unobservable cosmic force; the origin of all.

Edward Conklin

Chapter 14

*Ergo stercus accidit.*

Denouement

Philosophy, religion, and the sciences of physics and cosmology, each in their own way, conceptually and metaphorically point to the reality existence of an unseen but intuited cosmic force. Yet for the greater population, the advanced knowledge of these disciplines will remain difficult to comprehend.

In a lifetime many kinds of knowledge may be acquired by an individual. Many waste the potential of their lives by only obtaining a minimal level of education. Important areas of knowledge to acquire in life, is how to stay healthy, to be educated and skilled in a work career so as to earn a living, and to get along with family, friends, and coworkers. Of all the knowledge that can be obtained, the most important to acquire is to learn about that which moves all things into, through and out of existence. This is truly the most important knowledge.

All religions have been, and continue to be, varied attempts to comprehend and relate with the metaphysical origin of the environment and life. During many centuries of human evolution, the question of where did all things come from, was answered by general acceptance that all things came from a human-like god creator. While humans today continue to pray to a human-like god, this behavior is a waste of time and money. A god exists only as a human conceived idea or concept, that once accepted and often repeated in thoughts and words, is supported only by superficial faith and belief.

Theism is the shared false knowledge that a human-like god created and oversees human activities. A god is a comfortable cocoon that individuals spin with thoughts to surround themselves.

The popular view of a human-like is based merely on faith, belief, and tradition. The theistic view of a god is bolstered by widespread acceptance among the unthinking, seeking to obtain allied assistance to survive earthly life and an afterlife. Having a human-like god is a way to obtain ethical cooperation and compliance among humans. For example, the message of Judaism is that individual willing should follow the commandment laws. The most important tenet of Christianity is that willing to exist and to survive this biological life at the expense of another's well-being, is to be renounced and given up. Preference is given to subduing personal harmful egocentric willfulness. Only the willing of love and forgiveness on earth is acceptable behavior, and the individual is urged to look forward to an afterlife existence where a greater human-like father god rules. The religion of Islam says, humans should submit individual willing five times daily in prayer to the greater willing of Allah, who will eventually judge earthly human willing at the time of resurrection.

Theistic religion is an ideational effort to exist under the protection of a human-like god. Early feeble human intelligence conceived of and placed the protective blanket layer of a human-like god over themselves. Not knowing from what or how things have come into existence is where gods are tacked on as the human-like origin of the environment and living forms. The ego of a god is a product of a human religious group ego that thinks their own theistic concept is better than other cultures. For example, Judaism, Christianity, and Islam all share the same god, but the god chose to name his Jewish culture as the best among all the other peoples of the earth. (Deuteronomy 7:6).The same god gave Christians his only son Jesus to establish the true religion. The same god gave to Muhammad and the Islamic culture his special last words of communication. The ego of a god has been created by and reflects the collective importance of the egocentric culture.

The ego of a god reflects the ego-making process of humans, and therefore a god has many meanings. One meaning is that a god is an imagined model for human improvement. Humans have the potential for improvement, to be at peace, loving, creative, intelligent, and happy, rather than the usual human conditions of the opposite of these qualities.

Humans have the innate ability to improve and, dare I say, perfect themselves, and a human-like god is an empty symbol for that ability. This is especially so in the area of ethics. Humans are liars and are aggressive to fellow humans, especially in the fields of business, law, politics, government, and religion. Since this is the case, a deeply felt need for a higher role model is projected outward to be a god. A god is a regulator of human behavior, an authority figure humans can look to and emulate as a role model. Humans can imitate a god who is said to be loving, caring, and just; qualities the vast majority of humans lack.

Supposing an intelligent god to exist, also vicariously expands human ability to learn. Since a god knows everything there is to know, humans can seek to learn more as well. Human knowing is limited to sequences of time. The brain/mind continually transforms sensations into images and positions them in a space location and structures a time sequence. The detected sequence of change of objects is then structured into cause and effect. A god who is said to be all-knowing or omniscient, can supplement and assist human limited space and time, and cause and effect way of knowing. A god that knows about everything, can be appealed to, and can then reveal what he knows to humans through guidance, influence, and revelation.

There are many gods and goddesses as invisible helpers in so many differing cultures. They exist as there are not many human helpers that can control the environment and disease, and that can be depended upon for trust, truth, and mutual support. For theism, the unseen origin of existence is modeled on the human male who is physically taller and is above the female, is stronger and can better protect. But what a poor model for comprehending a metaphysical origin with use of such an immature and distorted anthropomorphic concept.

Humans need some stronger support than their individual frail human self which is vulnerable to accident, irrevocable mistakes that once done cannot be undone, and the excessive evil force of the environment, other life forms, and fellow humans.

Bewildered and overwhelmed at times with life, the majority of humankind slumps down to stare toward the sky and fill the unknown with the unreality of a human-like god.

Reaction Formation

A human-like god is born in the recesses of the human brain/ mind, evoked by both the fear of life and the fear of death. In life, there are fears of harm from animal and human aggression, disease, natural disasters, fear of aging, and from these experiences comes the fear of death. From experience of the fears of life and death, developed the defense mechanism of a psychological reaction formation in the human mind.

A human-like god is a reaction formation of the human mind, a response of emotion and thought to how existence really is. Having a god is an imaginary way of being safe in an unsafe and often unpredictable existence. For Sigmund Freud (1856-1939) and psychoanalysis, reaction formation is an unconscious defense mechanism to reduce anxiety by concealing one's true thoughts and feelings, and by thinking and behaving in an opposite way. When there is an emotion or thought that is too threatening or anxiety provoking, it can be unconsciously transformed into the opposite. This mechanism reduces and avoids awareness and expression of the threatening emotion or thought. Examples include, disliking someone but being unwilling to express this and reacting by being overly nice to the person, resulting in the concealing of one's true feelings of aggression. Another example is, being attracted to someone and denying those feelings by expressing dislike toward the person.

Similarly, with the reaction formation known as religion, the emotional anxiety of the unknown and fear of the struggle, conflict, and suffering of life is reduced and avoided. Those who accept the view of theistic religion agree with others that the origin of existence is human-like and good. In reality, the origin of existence is not human-like and is at best only half good. The origin of existence is a non-personal and uncaring cosmic force that prefers to go in circles and cycles, as it moves the environment and life into existence.

As a member of a patriarchal culture, the founder of Christianity used a simple father metaphor to be looked to as a shared symbol for where the environment and life has come from and to where human life is going. A father god is a symbol of ultimate parental caring. Christian popular art portrays Jesus and the saints looking outward and upward in the direction of a human-like god. In reality, their gaze should be directed downward and inward, to a cosmic immanence that move all things as inanimate movement and animate growth. That which moves a cosmos of galaxies, stars, sun, moon, and planets, is also equally animate within every living plant, animal, and human.

Pervading Force

There is no evidence for the existence of a human-like god as the origin of life, only faith, hope, and agreement with agreeable fellow theists. That which moves all things through existence is not a god, but a pervading cosmic force. To take an immediate now cosmic force and contrive a story of it to be human-like, is deserving of blame and censure. The maker of things is not human-like as portrayed in a story, but is an indestructible pervading force that moves relative forces, energy elements, environment, life, humans, and all things through existence. That which pervades and propels all things does so from outside and inside as a "go" force, not from a separate outside human-like god.

Knowing of the brain/mind is limited to space, time, and relative change of causality. Therefore, it is not possible to know what occurs beyond these limitations. There is an all-pervading cosmic force not subject to sensory space and time causal change and observation. This cosmic force neither comes into nor goes out of existence, yet it pervades and moves all other relative forces and energies.

The past is what was, the future is what will be, and the present is what has been pre-sent. Pre-sent by what, a human-like god or a pervading force of cause and effect change? There is zero evidence of a human-like god, but there exists overwhelming evidence for relative forces and energy elements of cause and effect change.

The cosmic parent of life is in reality a pervading force outside and is immanent inside life forms as function and growth.

A knowing human-like god did not create the environment and life, an unknowing cosmic force did. The unknowing environment of relative forces and energies of the universe has been estimated by cosmologists to exist for twelve to fourteen billion years. There is scientific evidence of physics for the evolution of elements from the first element of hydrogen into the other heavier ninety-four natural elements. There is also fossil evidence of physical and biological evolution over millions of years from simple to more complex forms of life and their eventual species extinction. A cosmic force moves elements of energy, galaxies, stars, planets and moons, in circles, having a beginning and an end, and also moves living forms in a circle, having a conception and death. An unknowing pervading cosmic force only moves all things, there is no caring for environmental or living forms that exist, only as a brief sojourn on the inevitable way out of existence.

Evolution

English naturalist Charles Darwin (1809–1882) participated on a five year around the earth voyage on the HMS Beagle. During his sojourn he observed the distribution and variation of plants and animals, and collected specimens and fossils of them. This led him to formulate his theory of life evolving over time from simpler to more complex and diverse life forms in a branching pattern of evolution based on the process of natural selection. In the year 1859, he published his scientific theory in the book, *On the Origin of Species*. Through presenting his observations and evidence, and discussing any anticipated objections to his theory, Darwin argued and convinced many in his own lifetime of the truth of evolution. His introduction to the theory of common descent and evolution states:

"As many more individuals of each species are born than can possibly survive; and as, consequently, there is a frequently recurring struggle for existence.

It follows that any being, if it vary however slightly in any manner profitable to itself, under the complex and sometimes varying conditions of life, will have a better chance of surviving, and thus be naturally selected. From the strong principle of inheritance, any selected variety will tend to propagate its new and modified form."

Darwin concludes his work with the words: "There is grandeur in this view of life, with its several powers, having been originally breathed into a few forms or into one; and that, whilst this planet has gone cycling on according to the fixed law of gravity, from so simple a beginning endless forms most beautiful and most wonderful have been, and are being, evolved."

In a 2013 survey conducted of thirty-four countries as to whether the theory of evolution is true, in the United States only forty percent accept evolution as true, twenty percent are not sure, and forty percent are convinced evolution theory is false. The USA ranks at the bottom thirty-three and only the country of Turkey ranks lower at number thirty-four in rejecting the truth of evolution. This is a scary, scary thought. Darwin's theory of evolution is still today just barely overthrowing Middle East fables of a human-like god. This progress is accelerated in Western Europe, and of course in Asia. Not until the early 1960s has evolution been accepted and widely taught in USA schools. The majority of citizens continue to indulge in the cognitively immature view of anthropomorphic theism.

While modern science realistically eliminates anthropomorphism from the origin of existence, science does not go so far as to accept the view of a metaphysical pervading and propelling force that cannot be measured. Instead, science insists on an observable and measurable cause of existence and has, since the 1950's, claimed it to be a natural Big Bang explosion, the effect of this is energy found to go in circles of elements. While science observes and pragmatically measures the reality of forces and energies, it ignores a greater reality of a metaphysical cosmic force with its theoretical thought measures of a Big Bang explosion, M theory, and concepts of smaller and smaller sought quantum particles.

When all god concepts are removed and all scientific measurable quantum particle theories are discarded, there remains only the intuitive reality of a metaphysical cosmological force. From a formless pervading cosmic force occurs a parting of relative force and particles into various parts of functions and forms. Quantum particles are by perforce, a continuation of a greater cosmic force, which explains how quantum particles can super-position and be entangled and nonlocal.

Human religion attempts to comprehend an all-pervading cosmic force by positing an arbitrary beginning and by placing a human-like god there. It was not a god's thought that brought all things into existence, it was human thoughts and words that brought a story of a human-like god into existence. Once upon a time god stories, come to be only through human effort to comprehend an ever-existent cosmic force. Yet no conceived story of a human-like god can match the daily display content of a cosmic reality.

Each particular god is a human creation, a symbol of assistance to help humans reduce or to escape suffering. A god is a way of getting humans to cooperate with each other with a promise of reward or threat of punishment. Those who worship and ask a god to do things for them, by so doing admit they are unable to accomplish a task on their own. Those who appeal to a god for special treatment waste their time, as a single cosmic force supports and moves all things equally without exception, both the moderation of good and the excesses of evil.

Everything opposes all other things. Humans oppose other humans, animals oppose animals, and plants oppose other plants. Said in myths to be beyond nature, super-nature gods oppose other gods, and gods oppose devils, and both gods and devils oppose humans. In reality, the originating cosmic force objectifies its presence, and by so doing goes in omni-moving circles and cycles of functions and forms.

Humans are in awe of the vastness of the universe. This in turn gives rise to important existential questions, such as: "How did the universe begin, and why is life a struggle and vulnerable to suffering?"

The traditional way to make plain an answer, is to conceive the presence of a human-like god.

Yet, by observing the continual change and motion of the environment and life, it is evident that an omni-moving cosmic force, is everywhere, outside and inside. The presence of a non-human-like cosmic force cannot be observed as a cause as it is not measurable. It has to be intuitively perceived by calming and quieting personal willing and knowing. This achieved, there can be experienced in the movement and involuntary change of the body, a direct identification with that which moves all things. The essence of existence is not something that knows, it is that which moves all things as an unseen and an unknowing pervading cosmic force.

That which moves billions of galaxies and stars, planets and moons, via the environment supports all life forms from outside and grows them from inside. Life moves without conscious thoughts, body cells and organs function, and the body self-heals and silently grows.

Struggle

Before and after a brief lifetime of this never to be again particular existence, there is a vast unknown with only a very slim faith to serve as a guide to an awesome all-pervading eternity. A god is a way of remaining optimistic on the way through a life of difficulties. Humans long for a place where there is no struggle, conflict, and suffering. In response to this longing, theistic religion teaches that there is such a place of peace. It is said that a soul survives the grueling process of life and physical death. Yet, in Judeo-Christian-Islamic view, the surviving soul must, if deserved, also face an afterlife of suffering inflicted as punishment by a human-like god.

To say a god has a better place for humans after a lifetime of struggle and suffering on the earth that he created, is to be blindly optimistic. With such a poor showing on earth can the afterlife be any better, a place where the good and evil angels were spawned in conflict to produce a Satan or Devil and where there is located the place of struggle, conflict, and suffering of a Hell?

"And there was war in heaven: Michael and his angels fought against the dragon; and the dragon fought and his angels, and prevailed not; neither was their place found any more in heaven. And the great dragon was cast out, that old serpent, called the Devil, and Satan, which deceiveth the whole world: he was cast out into the earth, and his angels were cast out with him." (Revelation 12:7-9)

Existence is a devilish struggle of conflict and suffering. One cosmic force is the origin of both good and evil experiences. Christian thought has fractured it into a good god and an evil opposing entity. A human-like god placed at the beginning of existence, above the present life, and at the time of death, is what humans use to overall explain what good there is in life. The serpent in the Garden that Christian theology regards as Satan, the Devil, and Lucifer, is merely a human symbol to explain the evil of life experience.

In the view of Western accepted Middle East religions, for some the suffering of life on earth is but a prelude to the dread of a future afterlife judgment, and potential of punishment for wrong doing. Humans are faced with the task to eke out some little good on the earth so as to avoid further future suffering in an afterlife. Of the future final Christian judgment and afterlife it is said:

"And I saw the dead, small and great, standing before God, and books were opened. And another book was opened, which is the Book of Life. And the dead were judged according to their works, by the things which were written in the books…And anyone not found written in the Book of Life was cast into the lake of fire." (Revelation 20:12, 15)

In theistic thinking, all of existence has been planned and designed but what can be said of such a planner, such a designer? Sadist? Insane? As told in the Garden of Eden story, the god cursed human life with the evil of struggle and suffering. Inflicted by the god from the very beginning, the god is eternally ready to inflict suffering on as many humans that deserve it during and after the ending of life.

God

The concept of a human-like god is the human attempt to give some time of temporary peace through the often difficult struggle to exist. Marooned in a life of ageing and eventual death, and based on need, the human mind manufactures a human-like god. The brain/mind seeks to navigate the body successfully through both life and after death. Facing the fears of life and inevitable death, most individuals cannot confidently rely on their own ability and knowledge but out of necessity and tradition, accept and rely on a human-like god.

Each individual through personal experience eventually and painfully learns of their own limitations of knowledge and ability to choose a successful course through life. The experience of limitation and pain is the pivot point on which many individuals turn from their own limited efforts to the imagined assistance of a human-like god. Only something greater than humans is capable of making existence worthwhile. The leap from limited personal effort to asking an imagined human-like god to intervene, requires a psychological maneuver known as faith. A god is an imagined talisman to help avoid mistakes, maintain balance, promote tolerance, and to aid in acceptance of harmful experiences of life as inevitable. Struggling psychologically and emotionally inside, and struggling with what is outside, a god most often appears in human thought to rescue the individual from the many challenges of life.

Safety

Early humans had to have been wondrously frightened of existence with its many unexpected diseases, accidents, storms, and aggression of animals and fellow humans. Conceived and born out of struggle and the will to live, out of the need to survive the dangers of the environment, the need for safety gave birth to a human-like god.

An additional dynamic for the origin of a god may be in human dream experience of deceased ancestors, probably accepted as continuing to exist in an ethereal afterlife dimension. Dreams may have been accepted as an afterlife realm with the deceased existing therein. Through time a particularly revered ancestor may have been promoted to the rank of a primal parent figure and worshiped as a god.

To accept the view of a greater human-like god effectively supports the human will to live and to survive calamities. To reduce the sense of being unsafe, optimism in the form of a human-like god was developed, and then taught to children. This keeps the tradition of a human-like god viable through generations. Yet, the view of a human-like god is harmful to instill in young children. Promoting the view of a god is an adult attempt to convince the young that existence is generally safe, when it is not. Life is deceptive; it seems to be generally safe but is frequently and unexpectedly punctuated with change and difficulties. Risk and dangers to life are not exceptions but the rule.

Most humans think of life as generally safe and have comfortable routines of family, work, eating, and errands. Most feel and expect to be safe but the unfolding course of events reveal life to not be so safe. If fortunate to reach maturity, most come to realize how dependent and vulnerable they are to conditions. Whether in childhood or adulthood, many are converted to the view of a human-like god who can assist during the challenges of life.

The intent and work of a religion is to make its members feel they are protected and safe from chance and harmful events. It takes effort to be alert and survive on one's own but with a god keeping guard, humans can relax to live with routine expectations of health and happiness. A god is said to have events well in hand under an ever alert and watchful eye, ready to respond, if the person deserves a response. Most often there is no response or relief. Hope is the continued clinging to good expectations that may or may not happen.

The true goal of a religious service should not be ritual, inspiration, or entertainment, but learning. Humankind has to learn that religion, as it exists today, is the cognitive artifact of a primitive attempt to find where the environment and life came from.

For the majority of the human population, the cosmic puzzle and riddle of existence continues and never gets solved. Instead, solace is sought in the popular imaginary view of a human-like god, who can respond to individual request for protection and relief.

Humans need a comforter and a mediate buffer between their individual self, the environment, animals, and other humans. A human-like god is said to be a helper to humans but is not much of a help to the environment, or to animals.

Both religion and science separate human beings from meaningful comprehension of life and human heritage. Religion limits and separates an individual from the environment by insisting on a human-like god that is unseen. Science limits and separates by an obsession to know objects through observation and measuring the size, and cause and effect behavior of phenomena.

The science of physics does have a theory of how a primary cosmic force transitions and parts into secondary mass particles as the building blocks of all inanimate and animate forms. Contemporary physicists speak of the Higgs (named for physicist Peter Higgs) boson, a hypothetical fundamental particle that is predicted to exist at the quantum level. Experiments to find the Higgs boson particle have been ongoing at the Large Hadron Collider utilized by the European Organization for Nuclear Research (CERN). In 2012 officials of the European Organization for Nuclear Research announced that physicists had identified the decay of the elusive boson particle, or at least identified a particle that matched predictions of how the boson should behave. Physicist Leon Lederman was the first to refer to the Higgs boson as the "god article." The Higgs boson is theorized to be the fundamental particle that contributes to other quantum particles to have mass, and to evolve into relative existence. However, other physicists' dislike that the public media refers to the Higgs boson particle as the "god particle," as by so doing the term suggests a human-like deity is involved. What the media is clumsily referring to, is the creative transition from a pure cosmic force, or Higgs Field, into the beginning of all relative existence.

Based on the Standard Model of particle physics, bosons are a transition from the pure force of perhaps dark matter present through all of space. Bosons enable particles of mass to form, and is the transition from a field to environmental and living forms. The Higgs field is a hypothetical quantum ground or field, ubiquitous or omnipresent.

The Higgs field has a non-zero value in its ground state, meaning it is a presence capable of transition into something, referred to as the Higgs boson, the fundamental particle that contributes to the mass of quarks and electrons. Higgs bosons are an elementary excitation, meaning they are transition effects from the ground state of the Higgs field.

Physics is efficient at observation and measuring. However, physics can never fully explain what the universe is, and how humans are connected to it by searching endlessly for the ultimate particle to measure. Aesthetic meditative perception that joins individual function with the unmeasurable related movement of the universe is needed to reveal the last piece of the puzzle of existence.

The environment and movement of living cells are a direct continuation of a metaphysical cosmic force of the universe. Unable to intuitively comprehend a continuum of motion from a metaphysical cosmic force into environmental and living forms, humans continue to falsely see a difference between material and spiritual, and animals and humans.

To fill this cognitive gap is where the ignorance of humankind produces a human-like god. Just as modern science attempts to observe and objectively measure everything possible, so does religion attempt with only thought to subjectively measure where things have come from with the conceived notion of a human-like god. The great majority of unthinking humans are unwilling to accept the view that the origin of existence is not human-like. The view that what brings all things into existence is not human-like, and is an impersonal cosmic force, will never quite be a useful tool for those who want the earth to be a special ethical place to live under the safe rule of a human-like god. Yet, true human ethics can only be grounded on perceiving one shared metaphysical origin of a cosmic force.

Heritage

Rather than limp along on their own, humans conceived a human-like god to better survive on earth and after physical death.

With an imaginary god, humans can live a better life by appealing for help, and there will be a human-like destination to get to at the unknown end of life. In theistic thinking, only a god can make a soul and save it from random destruction. Theistic humans cannot trust themselves to nonhuman-like nature, only to what is human-like.

The true genesis story of the twenty-first century is that all of life is heir to the environment. As environmental processes struggle and conflict one with another, this behavior is continued in the conscious and subconscious biological struggle of living forms. An indestructible pervading force moves the cosmos and has shaped the various forms of nonlife and life. There is a continuation of a metaphysical force present in the evolving reproduction process of life.

The English word nature is derived from Latin natus and nasci meaning, to be born, to come forth. The word is defined variously as:

"A creative and controlling force in the universe, the environment of the earth, weather functions, an inner force or forces in an individual as an inherent essential characteristic or innate genetic trait, a function of an organism or person, such as human nature."

The cosmos is a place of forces, energies, and relative continuous motion. The behavior of the cosmos is related and relative to human behavior. Human nature is a continuation of nature that is in turn a continuation of a cosmic force. Human nature does not come from a human-like god; human nature is born from the nature or environment of earth, in turn born from that which gives birth to all, a metaphysical cosmic force.

The English word human is derived from the Latin word humanus, in turn derived from the Latin word homo (belonging to the biological genus homo) that in turn is derived from the Indo-European Sanskrit word dhghem, meaning earth. An early view of humankind was that life came from the interior energy of the earth. Today it is known, through the theory and evidence of evolution that these early earth origin myths were correct, life did evolve from the environment.

Recent evidence also suggests that comets or meteorites may have brought life to planet earth where it continued to evolve dependent on the environment.

Cognitive Tool

For early evolving humans, existence was a problem to be solved through both physical and cognitive means. The making of stone tools is an ancient Paleolithic human activity dating from 2.5 million years ago. Stone tool making was a skill that enabled early humans to survive. Early humans are known for their early ability to make various stone tools of hand axes, scrapers, spears, hammers, and later, the bow and stone-tipped arrows.

In a similar way, late Neolithic humans conceptually constructed the cognitive rudimentary tool of a human-like god to explain existence and events occurring in the environment. A human-like god is a utilitarian conceptual tool to better assist humans to survive.

While stone tool making to aid in survival began at a much earlier time, a god is a fairly recent human made cognitive tool to survive existence. Similar to the continued finding of the remains of stone tools in the geologic layer, the artifact tool of a human-like god continues to be found today in the cognitive layers of the human brain/mind. The psychological mechanism of god making must be scrutinized, exposed to light, and laid bare. The cognitive distortion of a human-like god must be removed, and sound mental health restored.

A god is a conceived strategy to regulate human behavior for the better, a way of furnishing direction from a lower to a higher level. Whoever maintains the view of a human-like god, simply wants to improve themselves, and wants extra help doing so, even if imaginary. Yet judiciously, just as stone tools have become obsolete, so the cognitive tool of a human-like god is on its way to becoming obsolete. As did the use of stone tools, the cognitive tool of a human-like god is now rapidly receding into history.

www.ingramcontent.com/pod-product-compliance
Lightning Source LLC
Chambersburg PA
CBHW071422160426
43195CB00013B/1778